"*The Clean House*, a fresh, funny play by the talented Sarah Ruhl, breathes life into the phrase 'romantic comedy.' It is not, by any means, a traditional boy-meets-girl story. In fact, disease, death and dirt are among the subjects it addresses. This comedy is romantic, deeply so, but also visionary, tinged with fantasy, extravagant in feeling, maybe a little nuts. Ms. Ruhl's voice is an unusual one: astringent but compassionate, sardonic at times, at others ardently emotional. *The Clean House* is imbued with a melancholy but somehow comforting philosophy: that the messes and disappointments of life are as much a part of its beauty as romantic love and chocolate ice cream, and a perfect punch line can be as sublime as the most wrenchingly lovely aria."

—New York Times

"Touching, inventive, invigoratingly compact and luminously liquid, *Eurydice* reframes the ancient myth of ill-fated love to focus not on the bereaved musician but on his dead bride— and on her struggle with love beyond the grave."

—San Francisco Chronicle

"*Melancholy Play* mixes the absurdity of Pirandello and Fellini and the edgy prettiness of Edna St. Vincent Millay. Off-beat, lyrical and just a little bit nutty, it is a real charmer."

—Chicago Sun-Times

"*The Clean House* marks the arrival of a playwright with a unique comic voice, perspective and sense of theater. A wondrously mad and moving work."

—Variety

The
Clean
House

AND OTHER PLAYS

The
Clean
House

AND OTHER PLAYS

Sarah Ruhl

THEATRE COMMUNICATIONS GROUP
NEW YORK
2006

The Clean House and Other Plays is published by Theatre Communications Group, Inc., 520 Eighth Avenue, 24th Floor, New York, NY 10018-4156.

This publication is made possible in part with public funds from the New York State Council on the Arts, a State Agency.

TCG books are exclusively distributed to the book trade by Consortium Book Sales and Distribution, 1045 Westgate Drive, St. Paul, MN 55114.

LIBRARY OF CONGRESS CATALOGING-IN-PUBLICATION DATA
Ruhl, Sarah.
The clean house and other plays / Sarah Ruhl.—1st ed.
p. cm.
ISBN-13: 978-1-55936-266-5
ISBN-10: 1-55936-266-9
I. Title.
PS3618.U48C57   2006
8129.6—dc22   2006006833

Book design and composition by Lisa Govan
Cover design by Mark Melnick
Cover photo by Ralph Gibson

First Edition, September 2006
Third Printing, August 2007

To my first teacher, Kathy Ruhl.
Thank you for taking me to the theater.

Acknowledgments

I would be laboring in solitude without the help of my family. Thank you: Tony, Anna, Kate, Mom, Curt, Cecilia, Theo and the Kehoe clan, for making me laugh at myself. Thank you to Liz and the Charuvastra/Shells for baby-sitting while I go to rehearsals. And to the playwrights, poets and fiction writers who have offered their friendship, read drafts, shared tea and couches: Jacob Appel, Andy Bragen, Quill Camp, Julia Cho, Jorge Cortinas, Christine Evans, E. Tracy Grinnell, Beth Henley, Tina Howe, the Sewing Circle, Sherry Mason, Charlotte Meehan, Octavio Solis, Mark Tardi, Kathleen Tolan, Karen Zacarias, and all the folks at New Dramatists.

Thank you to the directors who I collaborated with on these plays in early drafts: Rebecca Brown, Richard Corley, Chris Fields, Daniel Fish, Davis McCallum, Kristin Newbom, Joyce Piven, Bill Rauch, Moisés Kaufman, Debbie Saivetz, Molly Smith, Rebecca Taichman, Jessica Thebus, Les Waters, Samuel West, Kate Whoriskey, and Mark Wing-Davey.

I also want to thank composers and designers who have made major contributions to my understanding of these plays. First, thanks to Christopher Steele-Nicholson, who taught me by example what it is to be an artist. Also, thank you to: Christopher Acebo, Scott Bradley, Andromache Chalfant, Michael Friedman, André Pluess, Bray Poor, Michael Roth, Jeffrey Weeter, and Darron L. West.

Thank you to theaters who bravely offered homes to these plays in early stages, for development or production: About Face Theatre, Arena Stage, Berkeley Repertory Theatre, the Goodman Theatre, the Lark Play Development Center, Lincoln Center Theater, Madison Repertory Theatre, the McCarter Theatre Center, Seattle Repertory Theatre, South Coast Repertory, Victory Gardens Theater, The Wilma Theater, Woolly Mammoth Theatre Company and Yale Repertory Theatre. Special thanks to the Piven Theatre, where Joyce Piven commissioned and produced my first play outside of a university. She put great faith in me, and taught me anything I might know about the melody of a line in an actor's mouth.

Many thanks to the dramaturgs and editors who have contributed to the life of these plays: André Bishop, Mark Bly, Liz Engleman, Lisa McNulty, Janice Paran, Rachel Rusch, Catherine Sheehy, Kathy Sova, Chris Sumption, and Craig Watson. Thank you to Bruce Ostler and Antje Oegel, who are secret dramaturgs and have helped these plays see the light of day.

Clearly these plays would not live without the actors who brought them to life. I want to thank all of you by thanking one in particular—who else could have played all these roles: Little Stone, Queen Elizabeth, Orlando, Eurydice, Tilly, and the Village Idiot. Only Polly Noonan.

Finally, I want to thank my teachers. To David Konstan and Joseph Pucci who made me love the ancients. To Mac Wellman for his rants, Nilo Cruz for his gentleness, and Maria Irene Fornes for her stark beauty. Most humbly, to Paula Vogel, for being the reason I started writing plays. And then being the reason I continued to write plays.

I wrote at least a portion of all of these plays when I lived on a street called Hope Street in Providence. I met my husband on Hope Street. Thank you Tony, for giving me the shelter and hope I needed to write these plays.

Table of Contents

The
Clean
House

*This play is dedicated
to the doctors in my life,
Tony and Kate*

PRODUCTION HISTORY

The first act of *The Clean House* was commissioned in 2000 by the McCarter Theatre Center in Princeton, NJ.

The world premiere production of *The Clean House*, in its full-length form, was produced by Yale Repertory Theatre (James Bundy, Artistic Director; Victoria Nolan, Managing Director) in New Haven, CT, on September 17, 2004. The production was directed by Bill Rauch; the set design was by Christopher Acebo, the lighting design was by Geoff Korf, the costume design was by Shigeru Yaji and the sound design and original music were by André Pluess (for information regarding the music, contact Bret Adams Ltd., Bruce Ostler, 448 West 44th Street, New York, NY 10036); the dramaturg was Rachel Rusch and the production stage manager was James Mountcastle. The cast was as follows:

LANE	Elizabeth Norment
MATILDE	Zilah Mendoza
VIRGINIA	Laurie Kennedy
A MAN/CHARLES	Tom Bloom
A WOMAN/ANA	Carmen de Lavallade and Franca M. Barchiesi

The Clean House was produced at the Goodman Theatre (Robert Falls, Artistic Director; Roche Schulfer, Executive Director) in Chicago on May 9, 2006. The production was directed by Jessica Thebus; the set design was by Todd Rosenthal, the lighting design was by James F. Ingalls, the costume design was by Linda Roethke and the sound design and original music were by André Pluess and Ben Sussman; the choreographer was Maria Lampert, the dramaturg was Tanya Palmer, the production stage manager was Joseph Drummond and the stage manager was T. Paul Lynch. The cast was as follows:

LANE	Mary Beth Fisher
MATILDE	Guenia Lemos
VIRGINIA	Christine Estabrook
CHARLES	Patrick Clear
ANA	Marilyn Dodds Frank

The Clean House will receive a production at Lincoln Center Theater (André Bishop, Artistic Director; Bernard Gersten, Executive Producer) in New York City on October 5, 2006. The production will be directed by Bill Rauch; with set design by Christopher Acebo, lighting design by James F. Ingalls, costume design by Shigeru Yaji and sound design and original music by André Pluess. The cast will include:

LANE	Blair Brown
MATILDE	Vanessa Aspillaga
VIRGINIA	Jill Clayburgh
CHARLES	John Dossett
ANA	Concetta Tomei

Characters

LANE: A doctor, a woman in her early fifties. She wears white.

MATILDE: Lane's cleaning lady, a woman in her late twenties. She wears black. She is Brazilian. She has a refined sense of deadpan.

VIRGINIA: Lane's sister, a woman in her late fifties.

CHARLES: Lane's husband, a man in his fifties. A compassionate surgeon. He is childlike underneath his white coat. In Act 1, Charles plays Matilde's father.

ANA: An Argentinean woman. She is impossibly charismatic. In Act 1, she plays Matilde's mother. She is older than Lane.

Note: Everyone in this play should be able to tell a really good joke.

Place

A metaphysical Connecticut. Or, a house that is not far from the sea and not far from the city.

Set

A white living room.
White couch, white vase, white lamp, white rug.
A balcony.

Note: The living room needn't be full of living room detail, though it should feel human. The space should transform and surprise. The balcony should feel high but also intimate—a close-up shot.

A Note on Pronunciation

"Matilde" is pronounced by the Americans in the play as "Matilda." It is pronounced by Ana as "Mathilda" at first, until Ana realizes that Matilde is Brazilian. And it is pronounced by Matilde, and the more observant characters in the play, as "Ma-chil-gee," which is the correct Brazilian pronunciation.

Note: See the end of the play for notes on subtitles and jokes.

A Note on Double Casting

It is important that Ana and Charles play Matilde's mother and father in Act 1. How much can they create, without speaking, a sense of memory and longing, through silence, gesture and dance? Ana's transformation at the very end of the play should create a full circle for Matilde, from the dead to the living and back again.

Act I

||||□||||
☰

1. Matilde

Matilde tells a long joke in Portuguese to the audience.
We can tell she is telling a joke even though we might not understand the language.
She finishes the joke.
She exits.

2. Lane

Lane, to the audience:

LANE

It has been such a hard month.
My cleaning lady—from Brazil—decided that she was depressed one day and stopped cleaning my house.
I was like: clean my house!
And she wouldn't!

We took her to the hospital and I had her medicated and she
Still Wouldn't Clean.
And—in the meantime—*I've* been cleaning my house!
I'm sorry, but I did not go to medical school to clean my own house.

3. Virginia

Virginia, to the audience:

VIRGINIA

People who give up the *privilege* of cleaning their own houses—
they're insane people.

If you do not clean: how do you know if you've made any progress
in life? I love dust. The dust always makes progress. Then I remove
the dust. That is progress.

If it were not for dust I think I would die. If there were no dust to
clean then there would be so much leisure time and so much
thinking time and I would have to do something besides thinking
and that thing might be to slit my wrists.

Ha ha ha ha ha ha just kidding.
I'm not a morbid person. That just popped out!

My sister is a wonderful person. She's a doctor. At an important
hospital. I've always wondered how one hospital can be more
important than another hospital. They are places for human
waste. Places to put dead bodies.

I'm sorry. I'm being morbid again.

My sister has given up the privilege of cleaning her own house.
Something deeply personal—she has given up. She does not know
how long it takes the dust to accumulate under her bed. She does
not know if her husband is sleeping with a prostitute because she
does not smell his dirty underwear. All of these things, she fails to
know.

I know when there is dust on the mirror. Don't misunderstand me—I'm an educated woman. But if I were to die at any moment during the day, no one would have to clean my kitchen.

4. Matilde

Matilde, to the audience:

MATILDE

The story of my parents is this. It was said that my father was the funniest man in his village. He did not marry until he was sixty-three because he did not want to marry a woman who was not funny. He said he would wait until he met his match in wit.

And then one day he met my mother. He used to say: your mother—and he would take a long pause— *(Matilde takes a long pause)* —is funnier than I am. We have never been apart since the day we met, because I always wanted to know the next joke.

My mother and father did not look into each other's eyes. They laughed like hyenas. Even when they made love they laughed like hyenas. My mother was old for a mother. She refused many proposals. It would kill her, she said, to have to spend her days laughing at jokes that were not funny.

Pause.

I wear black because I am in mourning. My mother died last year. Have you ever heard the expression: "I almost died laughing"? Well that's what she did. The doctors couldn't explain it. They argued. They said she choked on her own spit, but they don't really know. She was laughing at one of my father's jokes. A joke he took one year to make up, for the anniversary of their marriage. When my mother died laughing, my father shot himself. And so I came here, to clean this house.

5. Lane and Matilde

Lane enters.
Matilde is looking out the window.

LANE

Are you all right?

MATILDE

Yes.

LANE

Would you please clean the bathroom when you get a chance?

MATILDE

Yes.

LANE

Soon?

MATILDE

Yes.

Matilde looks at Lane.

LANE

The house is very dirty.

Matilde is silent.

This is difficult for me. I don't like to order people around. I've never had a live-in maid.

Matilde is silent.

Matilde—what did you do in your country before you came to the United States?

MATILDE

I was a student. I studied humor. You know—jokes.

LANE

I'm being serious.

MATILDE

I'm being serious too. My parents were the funniest people in Brazil. And then they died.

LANE

I'm sorry.
That must be very difficult.

MATILDE

I was the third funniest person in my family. Then my parents died, making me the first funniest. There was no one left to laugh at my jokes, so I left.

LANE

That's very interesting. I don't—always—understand the arts. Listen. Matilde. I understand that you have a life, an emotional life—and that you are also my cleaning lady. If I met you at—say—a party—and you said, I am from a small village in Brazil, and my parents were comedians, I would say, that's very interesting. You sound like a very interesting woman.

But life is about context.

And I have met you in the context of my house, where I have hired you to clean. And I don't want an interesting person to clean my house. I just want my house—cleaned.

Lane is on the verge of tears.

MATILDE

(With compassion) Is something wrong?

LANE

No, it's just that—I don't like giving orders in my own home. It makes me—uncomfortable. I want you to do all the things I want you to do without my having to tell you.

MATILDE

Do you tell the nurses at the hospital what to do?

LANE

Yes.

MATILDE

Then pretend I am your nurse.

LANE

Okay.
Nurse—would you polish the silver, please?

MATILDE

A doctor does not say: Nurse—would you polish the silver, please?
A doctor says: Nurse—polish the silver!

LANE

You're right. Nurse—polish the silver!

MATILDE

Yes, Doctor.

Matilde gets out silver polish and begins polishing.
Lane watches her for a moment, then exits.

6. Matilde

Matilde stops cleaning.

MATILDE

This is how I imagine my parents.

Music.
A dashing couple appears.

They are dancing.
They are not the best dancers in the world.
They laugh until laughing makes them kiss.
They kiss until kissing makes them laugh.

They dance.
They laugh until laughing makes them kiss.
They kiss until kissing makes them laugh.
Matilde watches.
Matilde longs for them.

7. Virginia and Matilde

The doorbell rings.
The music stops.
Matilde's parents exit.
They blow kisses to Matilde.
Matilde waves back.
The doorbell rings again.
Matilde answers the door.
Virginia is there.

MATILDE

Hello.

VIRGINIA

Hello. You are the maid?

MATILDE

Yes.
You are the sister?

VIRGINIA

Yes.
How did you know?

MATILDE

I dusted your photograph.
My boss said: this is my sister. We don't look alike.
I thought: you don't look like my boss. You must be her sister.
My name is Matilde. *(Brazilian pronunciation of Matilde: Ma-chil-gee)*

VIRGINIA

I thought your name was Matilde. *(American pronunciation of Matilde: Matilda)*

MATILDE

Kind of.

VIRGINIA

Nice to meet you.

MATILDE

Nice to meet you. I don't know your name.

VIRGINIA

Oh! My name is Virginia.

MATILDE

Like the state?

VIRGINIA

Yes.

MATILDE

I've never been to Virginia.

VIRGINIA

Maybe I should go.

MATILDE

To Virginia?

VIRGINIA

No. I mean, am I interrupting you?

MATILDE

No. I was just—cleaning. Your sister is at work.

VIRGINIA

She's always at work.

MATILDE

Would you like to come in?

VIRGINIA

Yes. Actually—I came to see you.

They enter the living room.

Lane tells me that you've been feeling a little blue.

MATILDE

Blue?

VIRGINIA

Sad.

MATILDE

Oh. She told you that?

VIRGINIA

Come, sit on the couch with me.

MATILDE

Okay.

Virginia goes to sit on the couch.
She pats the couch.
Matilde sits down next to her.

VIRGINIA

Do you miss home?

MATILDE

Of course I do. Doesn't everyone?

VIRGINIA

Is that why you've been sad?

MATILDE

No. I don't think so. It's just that—I don't like to clean houses. I think it makes me sad.

VIRGINIA

You don't like to clean houses.

MATILDE

No.

VIRGINIA

But that's so simple!

MATILDE

Yes.

VIRGINIA

Why don't you like to clean?

MATILDE

I've never liked to clean. When I was a child I thought: if the floor is dirty, look at the ceiling. It is always clean.

VIRGINIA

I like cleaning.

MATILDE

You do? Why?

VIRGINIA

It clears my head.

MATILDE

So it is, for you, a religious practice?

VIRGINIA

No. It's just that: cleaning my house—makes me feel clean.

MATILDE

But you don't clean other people's houses. For money.

VIRGINIA

No—I clean my own house.

MATILDE

I think that is different.

VIRGINIA

Do you feel sad *while* you are cleaning? Or before? Or after?

MATILDE

I am sad when I think about cleaning. But I try not to think about cleaning while I am cleaning. I try to think of jokes. But sometimes the cleaning makes me mad. And then I'm not in a funny mood. And *that* makes me sad. Would you like a coffee?

VIRGINIA

I would *love* some coffee.

> *Matilde goes to get a cup of coffee from the kitchen.*
> *Virginia takes stock of her sister's dust.*
> *Virginia puts her finger on the tabletops to test the dust.*
> *Then she wipes her dirty finger on her skirt.*
> *Then she tries to clean her skirt but she has nothing to clean it with.*
> *Matilde comes back and gives her the coffee.*

Thank you.

MATILDE

You're welcome.

Virginia drinks the coffee.

VIRGINIA

This is good coffee.

MATILDE

We make good coffee in Brazil.

VIRGINIA

Oh—that's right. You do!

MATILDE

Does that help you to place me in my cultural context?

VIRGINIA

Lane didn't describe you accurately.
How old are you?

MATILDE

Young enough that my skin is still good.
Old enough that I am starting to think: is my skin still good?
Does that answer your question?

VIRGINIA

Yes. You're twenty-seven.

MATILDE

You're good.

VIRGINIA

Thank you.
Listen. Matilde. *(American pronunciation)*

MATILDE

Matilde. *(Brazilian pronunciation)*

VIRGINIA

Yes.
I have a proposition for you.

MATILDE

A proposition?

VIRGINIA

A deal.
I like to clean. You do not like to clean. Why don't I clean for you?

MATILDE

You're joking.

VIRGINIA

No.

MATILDE

I don't get it. What do you want from me?

VIRGINIA

Nothing.

MATILDE

Then—why?

VIRGINIA

I have my house cleaned by approximately 3:12 every afternoon.
I have folded the corner of every sheet. The house is quiet. The
gold draperies are singing a little lullaby to the ottoman. The sil-
verware is gently sleeping in its box. I tuck in the forks, the
spoons, the knives. I do not have children.

MATILDE

I'm sorry.

VIRGINIA

(With increasing velocity) Don't be sorry. My husband is barren. Is
that the right word for a man? I never thought that the world was
quite good enough for children anyway. I didn't trust myself to
cope with how sick and ugly the world is and how beautiful children are, and the idea of watching them grow into the dirt and

mess of the world—someone might kidnap them or rape them or otherwise trample on their innocence, leaving them in the middle of the road, naked, in some perverse sexual position, to die, while strangers rode past on bicycles and tried not to look. I've thought about doing some volunteer work, but I don't know who to volunteer for.

A pause. She looks at Matilde.

Since I was twenty-two, my life has gone downhill, and not only have I not done what I wanted to do, but I have lost the qualities and temperament that would help me reverse the downward spiral—and now I am a completely different person.

I don't know why I am telling you all of this, Mathalina.

Matilde thinks about correcting Virginia. She doesn't.

MATILDE

Go on.

VIRGINIA

I used to study Greek literature. One summer my husband and I went to Europe. It was supposed to be relaxing but I have trouble relaxing on vacations. We were going to see ruins and I was going to write about ruins but I found that I had nothing to say about them. I thought: why doesn't someone just sweep them up! Get a very large broom!

I'm sorry. I was trying to say . . .

MATILDE

You were telling me how your life has gone downhill since you were twenty-two.

VIRGINIA

Yes. The point is: every day my house is cleaned by three o'clock. I have a lot of—time.

I'd be very happy to come here and clean Lane's house before Lane gets home from work. That is what I'm telling you. Only don't tell her. She wouldn't like it.

MATILDE

I will let you clean the house if it will make you feel better.

VIRGINIA

Let's start in the bathroom. I love cleaning the toilet. It's so dirty, and then it's so clean!

8. Lane and Matilde

Matilde is reading the funny papers.
Lane enters.

LANE

It's so clean!

MATILDE

Yes.

LANE

The medication is helping?

MATILDE

I'm feeling much better.

LANE

Well—that's terrific.

> *Lane exits.*
> *Matilde takes out her medication.*
> *She undoes the bottle,*
> *takes one pill out,*
> *looks at it,*
> *and throws it in the garbage can.*

9. Matilde

Matilde, to the audience:

MATILDE

The perfect joke makes you forget about your life. The perfect joke makes you remember about your life. The perfect joke is stupid when you write it down. The perfect joke was not made up by one person. It passed through the air and you caught it. A perfect joke is somewhere between an angel and a fart.

This is how I imagine my parents:

> *Music.*
> *Matilde's mother and father appear.*
> *They sit at a café.*

My mother and father are at a café.
My mother is telling my father a joke.
It is a dirty joke.
My father is laughing so hard that he is banging his knee on the underside of the table.
My mother is laughing so hard that she spits out her coffee.
I am with them at the café. I am eight years old.
I say: what's so funny?
(I *hate* not understanding a joke.)
My mother says: ask me again when you're thirty.
Now I'm almost thirty. And I'll never know the joke.

> *Matilde's mother and father look at her.*
> *They exit.*

10. Virginia and Matilde

The next day.
Virginia folds laundry.
Matilde watches.
Virginia is happy to be cleaning.

MATILDE

You're good at that.

VIRGINIA

Thank you.

MATILDE

You want to hear a joke?

VIRGINIA

Not really.

MATILDE

Why?

VIRGINIA

I don't like to laugh out loud.

MATILDE

Why?

VIRGINIA

I don't like my laugh. It's like a wheeze. Someone once told me that. Who was it—my husband? Do you have a husband?

MATILDE

No.

VIRGINIA

That's good.

MATILDE

Do you like your husband?

VIRGINIA

My husband is like a well-placed couch. He takes up the right amount of space. A man should not be too beautiful. Or too good in bed. A man should be—functional. And well chosen. Otherwise you're in trouble.

MATILDE

Does he make you laugh?

VIRGINIA

Oh no. Something uncontrollable would come out of my mouth
when he wanted it to. I wouldn't like that.

MATILDE

A good joke cleans your insides out. If I don't laugh for a week, I feel
dirty. I feel dirty now, like my insides are rotting.

VIRGINIA

Someone should make you laugh. I'm not the person to do it.

MATILDE

Virginia. My mother once said to me: Matilde, in order to tell a
good joke, you have to believe that your problems are very small,
and that the world is very big. She said: if more women knew more
jokes, there would be more justice in this world.

Virginia thinks about that.
Virginia comes across a white pair of women's underwear.
Matilde watches.

VIRGINIA

I've never seen my sister's underwear before.

MATILDE

Her underwear is practical. And white.

Virginia continues to fold underwear.

VIRGINIA

I wonder if Lane has gone through menopause yet. Her underwear
is very white. Some women throw out underwear when they get
a bloodstain. Other women keep washing the stain.

MATILDE

I can't afford to throw away underwear. If I could, believe me, I would. I would buy new underwear every day: purple, red, gold, orange, silver . . .

Virginia folds a pair of men's underwear.

VIRGINIA

It's a little weird to be touching my brother-in-law's underwear. He's a very handsome man.
When he and Lane first met, I thought: Lane gets the best of everything. A surgeon. With a specialty. He's—charismatic.

Virginia touches her brother-in-law's underwear as she folds.

Then I thought: it's better to have a husband who is not *too* handsome. Then you don't worry about him.

Virginia comes across a pair of women's black underwear.

These don't look like Lane.

MATILDE

No.

VIRGINIA

Too shiny

MATILDE

Too sexy.

Matilde and Virginia look at each other.

11. Lane and Virginia Have Coffee

Lane and Virginia have coffee in the living room.

VIRGINIA

The house is so clean!

LANE

Thanks.

VIRGINIA

It's working out—with your maid? What's her name?

LANE

(American pronunciation) Matilde.

VIRGINIA

That's right: Matilde. *(American pronunciation)*
Don't they say Matilde *(Brazilian pronunciation)* in Brazil?

LANE

I don't know.

VIRGINIA

I think they do.

LANE

How would you know?

Virginia shrugs.

VIRGINIA

Mmm . . .

LANE

Well, I'm sure she would tell me if I were saying her name wrong.
Anyway. She seems much better. How are you?

VIRGINIA

Oh, fine.
How's Charles?

LANE

Why do you ask?

VIRGINIA

No reason.

LANE

He's fine.

VIRGINIA

That's good. The last time I saw Charles was Christmas. You both work so hard.

LANE

He's been doing nine surgeries a day—we hardly see each other. I mean, of course we see each other, but, you know how it is. More coffee?

VIRGINIA

No, thanks.

LANE

Matilde! Could you clear these, please?

Matilde enters.

MATILDE

(To Virginia) Your cup, miss?

VIRGINIA

Oh, I'll get it—

Matilde winks at Virginia.
Matilde clears the plates.

Thanks.

MATILDE

Did everyone like their coffee?

LANE AND VIRGINIA

Yes.

MATILDE

Good.

Matilde exits.

LANE

Oh. That's Matilde. Sorry. That was rude. I should have introduced you. Or is it rude? Do you introduce the maid to the company?

VIRGINIA

I'm not the company. I'm your sister.

LANE

You're right.
I should have introduced you. I can't get used to having another person in the house.

VIRGINIA

Mmm. Yes. It must make you uncomfortable to—I don't know— read a magazine while someone cleans up after you.

LANE

I don't read magazines, Virginia. I go to work exhausted and I come home exhausted. That is how most of the people in this country function. At least people who have jobs.

A pause.
For a moment,
Lane and Virginia experience
a primal moment during which they
are seven and nine years old,
inside the mind, respectively.
They are mad.
Then they return quite naturally
to language, as adults do.

Sorry—I didn't mean—

VIRGINIA

I know.

At the same time:

VIRGINIA	LANE
Are you—?	I keep meaning to—

VIRGINIA

What?

LANE

Oh—it's just—I keep meaning to have you two over for dinner.
It's ridiculous—living so close and never seeing each other.

VIRGINIA

You're right. Maybe next week?

LANE

Next week is crazy. But soon.

Virginia nods.

12. Lane and Matilde

Night.
Matilde tries to think up the perfect joke.
Matilde looks straight ahead,
in the dark, in the living room.
She thinks.
Lane comes home from work.
She turns a light on.

LANE

Oh! You startled me.

MATILDE

You startled me, too.

LANE

What are you doing in the dark?

MATILDE

I was trying to think up a joke.
Almost had one.
Now it's gone.

LANE

Oh—well—can you get it back again?

MATILDE

I doubt it.

LANE

Oh.
Is Charles home?

MATILDE

No.

LANE

Did he call?

MATILDE

(With compassion) No.

LANE

Oh, well, he's probably just sleeping at the hospital.

Matilde is silent.

Sometimes there's no time to call home from the hospital. You're going from patient to patient, and it's—you know—crazy. When we were younger—Charles and I—we would page each other, we had this signal—two for good night—and three for—well, I don't know why I'm thinking about this right now. The point is—when you get older, you just *know* that a person is thinking of you, and working hard, and thinking of you, and you don't need them to call anymore. Since Charles and I are both doctors we both—understand—how it is.

MATILDE

Mmm.

LANE

Well, good night.

MATILDE

Good night.

LANE

Are you going to—just—sit here in the dark?

MATILDE

I might stay up a little longer to—what's the word?—tidy up.

LANE

Oh. Great. Just shut the light off when you—

Matilde turns the light off.

Oh. Good night.

MATILDE

Good night.

Lane exits.
Matilde tries to think up the perfect joke.
She closes her eyes.
The lights around her go from night to day
as she composes.

13. Virginia and Matilde. Then Lane.

Virginia enters.
Matilde opens her eyes.
Virginia irons.
Matilde watches.

MATILDE

I have a really good joke coming.

VIRGINIA

That's good.

MATILDE

You know how most jokes go in threes? Like this: Da da DA. I'm making up one that goes in sixes: Da da Da, da da DA.

VIRGINIA

I didn't know jokes had time signatures.

MATILDE

Oh, they do. Ask me what my profession is then ask me what my greatest problem is.

VIRGINIA

What's your profession?

MATILDE

I'm a comedian.

VIRGINIA

What's your—

MATILDE

Timing.

VIRGINIA

That's good.

MATILDE

But you're not laughing.

VIRGINIA

I'm laughing on the inside.

MATILDE

Oh. I like it better when people laugh on the outside.
I'm looking for the perfect joke, but I'm afraid if I found it, it would
kill me.

Virginia comes upon a pair of women's red underwear.

VIRGINIA

My God!

MATILDE

Oh . . .
No— *(As in—he wouldn't dare)*

VIRGINIA

No.

MATILDE

But— *(As in—he might dare)*

VIRGINIA

Do you think—here—in the house?

MATILDE

Maybe a park. I bet he puts them in his pocket, afterwards, and
forgets, because he's so happy. And then she's walking around for
the day, with no underwear, and you know what? She probably
likes it.

VIRGINIA

I hope it's not a nurse. It's such a cliché.

MATILDE

If she's a nurse, they would pass each other in the hospital, and she would say: hello, Doctor. And she knows, and he knows: no underwear.

VIRGINIA

No underwear in a *hospital*? It's unsanitary.

MATILDE

Or—maybe he just *likes* women's underwear. He might try them on.

VIRGINIA

Charles? No!

MATILDE

It's possible. You don't like to think about it, because he's your brother-in-law, but these things happen, Virginia. They do.

Lane enters.
Virginia quickly puts down the iron and sits.
Matilde stands and begins to iron badly.
Virginia hides the red underwear.

LANE

(To Virginia) What are you doing here?

VIRGINIA

Nothing.
How was work?

Lane moves to the kitchen.

Where are you going?

LANE

I'm going in the other room to shoot myself.

VIRGINIA

You're joking, right?

LANE

(From the kitchen) Right.

> *Matilde and Virginia look at each other.*
> *Matilde folds underwear.*
> *Virginia sits.*
> *Virginia stands.*
> *Virginia sits.*
> *Virginia stands.*
> *Virginia has a deep impulse to order the universe.*
> *Virginia arranges objects on the coffee table.*
> *Lane enters.*
> *Her left hand is bleeding.*
> *She holds it with a dish towel.*

VIRGINIA

Lane—what—are you—?

LANE

I'm disguising myself as a patient.

VIRGINIA

That's not funny.

LANE

I cut myself.

> *They look at her, alarmed.*

Don't worry. Even my wounds are superficial.

VIRGINIA

Lane?

LANE

Can opener. I was making a martini.

VIRGINIA

Why do you need a can opener to make a martini?

LANE

I didn't have the right kind of fucking olives, okay? I only have black olives! In a fucking can.

VIRGINIA

Lane?

LANE

He's gone off with a patient.

VIRGINIA

What?

LANE

His patient.

MATILDE

Oh . . .

LANE

Yes.

Virginia and Matilde glance toward the red underwear and look away.

VIRGINIA

Was it a—?

LANE

Mastectomy. Yes.

VIRGINIA

Wow. That's very—

LANE

Generous of him?

MATILDE

(To Virginia) A mastectomy?

Virginia gestures toward her breast.
Matilde nods.

VIRGINIA

How old is she?

LANE

Sixty-seven.

VIRGINIA AND MATILDE

Oh!

LANE

What?

VIRGINIA

Not what I expected.

LANE

A young nurse? The maid? No. He's in love.

VIRGINIA

But——with an older woman?

LANE

Yes.

VIRGINIA

I'm almost——impressed. She must have substance.

LANE

She's not a doctor.

VIRGINIA

Well, most men in his position . . . he's still——so——good-looking . . .

LANE

Virginia!

VIRGINIA

Sorry.

LANE

I've never been jealous, I've never been suspicious. I've never thought any other woman was my equal. I'm the best doctor. I'm the smartest, the most well-loved by my patients. I'm athletic. I have poise. I've aged well. I can talk to *anyone* and be on equal footing. How, I thought, could he even *look* at anyone else. It would be absurd.

VIRGINIA

Wow. You really are——confident.

LANE

I was blind. He didn't want a doctor. He wanted a housewife.

A pause.
Lane looks around the house.
She sees the objects on the coffee table—
a vase, some magazines, forcefully arranged.
She sees Matilde folding laundry, badly.

(To Virginia) Have you been cleaning my house?

Virginia and Matilde look at each other.
Matilde stops folding laundry.

VIRGINIA

No, I haven't been cleaning your house.

LANE

Those objects on the coffee table—that is how you arrange objects.

Virginia looks at the coffee table.

VIRGINIA

I don't know what you mean.

LANE

Matilde—has Virginia been cleaning the house?

VIRGINIA

I said no.

LANE

I asked Matilde.
Has Virginia been cleaning the house?

MATILDE

Yes.

LANE

For how long?

MATILDE

Two weeks.

LANE

You're fired.

A pause.

You're both fired.

VIRGINIA

You can't do that.
This is my fault.

LANE

I'm *paying* her to clean my house!

VIRGINIA

And your house is clean!

LANE

This has nothing to do with you, Virginia.

VIRGINIA

This has *everything* to do with me.

LANE

Matilde—do you have enough money saved for a plane ticket back home?

MATILDE

No.

LANE

You can stay one more week. I will buy you a plane ticket.

VIRGINIA

Lane. Your husband left you today.

LANE

I'm aware of that.

VIRGINIA

You're not capable of making a rational decision.

LANE

I'm always capable of making a rational decision!

MATILDE

You don't need to buy me a plane ticket. I'm moving to New York to become a comedian. I only need a bus ticket.

VIRGINIA

(To Lane) You can't do this!

LANE

I will not have you cleaning my house, just because the maid is depressed—

VIRGINIA

She's not depressed. She doesn't like to clean! It makes her sad.

Lane looks at Matilde.

LANE

Is that true?

MATILDE

Yes.

LANE

So—
then—
(To Virginia) why?

VIRGINIA

I don't know.

LANE

You looked through my things.

VIRGINIA

Not really.

LANE

I find this—incomprehensible.

VIRGINIA

Can't I do a nice thing for you without having a *motive*?

LANE

No.

VIRGINIA

That's—

LANE

You have better things to do than clean my house.

VIRGINIA

Like what?

LANE

I—

VIRGINIA

Like what?

LANE

I don't know.

VIRGINIA

No, you don't know.
I wake up in the morning, and I wish that I could sleep through the whole day, but there I am, I'm awake.

So I get out of bed. I make eggs for my husband. I throw the eggshells in the disposal. I listen to the sound of delicate eggshells being ground by an indelicate machine. I clean the sink. I sweep the floor. I wipe coffee grounds from the counter.

I might have done something different with my life. I might have been a scholar. I might have described one particular ruin with the cold-blooded poetry of which only a first-rate scholar is capable. Why didn't I?

LANE

I don't know.

VIRGINIA

I wanted something—big. I didn't know how to ask for it.
Don't blame Matilde. Blame me. I wanted—a task.

LANE

I'm sorry.
I don't know what to say.
Except:
(To Matilde) you're fired.

VIRGINIA

It's not her fault! You can't do this.

LANE

(To Virginia) What would you like me to do?

VIRGINIA

Let me . . . take care of you.

LANE

I don't need to be taken care of.

VIRGINIA

Everybody needs to be taken care of.

LANE

Virginia. I'm all grown-up.
I DO NOT WANT TO BE TAKEN CARE OF.

VIRGINIA

WHY NOT?

LANE

I don't want my sister to clean my house. I want a stranger to clean my house.

Virginia and Lane look at Matilde.

MATILDE

It's all right. I'll go.
I'll pack my things.
Good-bye, Virginia.
Good luck finding a task.

She embraces Virginia.

Good-bye, Doctor.
Good luck finding your husband.

She exits.
Lane and Virginia look at each other.

14. Lane. Then Matilde. Then Virginia.

Lane, to the audience:

LANE

This is how I imagine my ex-husband and his new wife.

Charles and Ana appear.
He undoes her gown.
Is it a hospital gown or a ball gown?

My husband undoes her gown.
He is very gentle.
He kisses her right breast.

Charles kisses Ana's right breast.

He kisses the side of it.
He kisses the shadow.
He kisses her left torso.

He kisses her left torso.

He kisses the scar,

He kisses the scar.

the one he made.
It's a good scar.
He's a good surgeon.
He kisses her mouth.
He kisses her forehead.
It's a sacred ritual, and
I hate him.

Matilde enters with her suitcase.
The lovers remain.

*They continue to kiss one another
on different body parts, a ritual.*

MATILDE

Is there anything else before I go?

LANE

No. Thank you.

MATILDE

Who are they?

LANE

My husband and the woman he loves. Don't worry. It's only my imagination.

MATILDE

They look happy.

LANE

Yes.

MATILDE

People imagine that people who are in love are happy.

LANE

Yes.

MATILDE

That is why, in your country, people kill themselves on Valentine's Day.

LANE

Yes.

MATILDE

Love isn't clean like that. It's dirty. Like a good joke. Do you want to hear a joke?

LANE

Sure.

Matilde tells a joke in Portuguese.

Is that the end?

MATILDE

Yes.

LANE

Was it funny?

MATILDE

Yes. It's not funny in translation.

LANE

I suppose I should laugh then.

MATILDE

Yes.

Lane tries to laugh.
She cries.

You're crying.

LANE

No, I'm not.

MATILDE

I think that you're crying.

LANE

Well—yes. I think I am.

Lane cries.
She laughs.
She cries.

She laughs.
And this goes on for some time.
Virginia enters.

VIRGINIA

Charles is at the door.

LANE

What?

VIRGINIA

Charles. In the hall.

MATILDE

Oh . . .

LANE

You let him in?

VIRGINIA

What could I do?
And—there's a woman with him.

LANE

In the *house?*

VIRGINIA

Yes.

LANE

What does she look like?
Is she pretty?

VIRGINIA

No.
(With a sense of apology) She's beautiful.

LANE

Oh.

From offstage:

CHARLES

Lane?

The women look at each other.
Blackout.
Intermission.

ACT 2

The white living room has become a hospital.
Or the idea of a hospital.
There is a balcony above the white living room.

1. Charles Performs Surgery
on the Woman He Loves

Ana lies under a sheet.
Beautiful music.
A subtitle projects: Charles Performs Surgery on the Woman He Loves.
Charles takes out surgical equipment.
He does surgery on Ana.
It is an act of love.
If the actor who plays Charles is a good singer,
it would be nice if he could sing
an ethereal medieval love song in Latin
about being medically cured by love
as he does the surgery.

If the actress who plays Ana is a good singer,
it would be nice if she recovered from the surgery
and slowly sat up and sang a contrapuntal melody.
When the surgery is over,
Charles takes off Ana's sheet.
Underneath the sheet,
she is dressed in a lovely dress.
They kiss.

2 . Ana

Ana, to the audience:

ANA

I have avoided doctors my whole life.
I don't like how they smell. I don't like how they talk. I don't admire their emotional lives. I don't like how they walk. They walk very fast to get somewhere—tac tac tac—I am walking somewhere important. I don't like that. I like a man who saunters. Like this.

Ana saunters across the stage like a man.

But with Charles, it was like—BLAM!
My mind was going: you're a doctor, I hate you.
But the rest of me was gone, walking out the door, with him.
When he performed surgery on me,
we were already in love.
I was under general anesthetic but I could sense him there.
I think he put something extra in—during the surgery.
Into the missing place.
There are stories of surgeons who leave things inside the body by mistake:
rubber gloves, sponges, clamps—
But—you know—I think Charles left his soul inside me.
Into the missing place.

She touches her left breast.

3. Charles

Charles, to the audience:

CHARLES

There are jokes about breast surgeons.
You know—something like—I've seen more breasts in this city than—
I don't know the punch line.
There must be a punch line.

I'm not a man who falls in love easily. I've been faithful to my wife. We fell in love when we were twenty-two. We had plans. There was justice in the world. There was justice in love. If a person was good enough, an equally good person would fall in love with that person. And then I met—Ana. Justice had nothing to do with it.

There once was a very great American surgeon named Halsted. He was married to a nurse. He loved her—immeasurably. One day Halsted noticed that his wife's hands were chapped and red when she came back from surgery. And so he invented rubber gloves. For her. It is one of the great love stories in medicine. The difference between inspired medicine and uninspired medicine is love.

When I met Ana, I knew:
I loved her to the point of invention.

4. Charles and Ana

CHARLES

I'm afraid that you have breast cancer.

ANA

If you think I'm going to cry, I'm not going to cry.

CHARLES

It's normal to cry—

ANA

I don't cry when I'm supposed to cry.
Are you going to cut it off?

CHARLES

You must need some time—to digest—

ANA

No. I don't need time. Tell me everything.

CHARLES

You have a variety of options. Many women don't opt for a mastectomy. A lumpectomy and radiation can be just as effective as—

ANA

I want you to cut it off.

CHARLES

You might want to talk with family members—with a husband—
are you married?—or with—

ANA

Tomorrow.

CHARLES

Tomorrow?

ANA

Tomorrow.

CHARLES

I'm not sure I have any appointments open tomorrow—

ANA

I'd like you to do it tomorrow.

CHARLES

Then we'll do it tomorrow.

They look at each other.
They fall in love.

ANA

Then I'll see you tomorrow, at the surgery.

CHARLES

Good-bye, Ana.

ANA

Good-bye.

They look at each other.
They fall in love some more.

Am I going to die?

CHARLES

No. You're not going to die.
I won't let you die.

They fall in love completely.
They kiss wildly.

What's happening?

ANA

I don't know.

CHARLES

This doesn't happen to me.

ANA

Me neither.

CHARLES

Ana, Ana, Ana, Ana . . . your name goes backwards and forwards
. . . I love you . . .

ANA

And I love you.
Take off your white coat.

They kiss.

5. Lane, Virginia, Matilde, Charles and Ana

We are back in the white living room.
We are deposited at the end of the last scene of the first act.
Charles is at the door, with Ana.

CHARLES

Lane?

LANE

Charles.

CHARLES

Lane. I want us all to know each other. I want to do things right,
from the beginning. Lane: this is Ana. Ana: this is my wife, Lane.

ANA

Nice to meet you. I've heard wonderful things about you. I've
heard that you are a wonderful doctor.

LANE

Thank you.

Ana holds out her hand to Lane.
Lane looks around in disbelief.
Then Lane shakes Ana's hand.

CHARLES

This is my sister-in-law, Virginia.

ANA

Hello.

VIRGINIA

How do you do.

MATILDE

(To Ana) You look like my mother.

ANA

Ah!

LANE

(To Ana) This is the maid, Matilde.
(To Charles) I fired her this morning.

ANA

Encantada, Matilde.
(Nice to meet you, Matilde.)

MATILDE

Encantada. Sou do Brasil.
(Nice to meet you. I'm from Brazil.)

ANA

Ah! Eu falo um pouco de portugues, mas falo mal.
(I know a little bit of Portuguese, but it's bad.)

MATILDE

Eh! boa tentativa! 'ta chegando la!
Es usted de Argentina?
*(Ah! Good try! Not bad!
You're from Argentina?)*

ANA

(In Spanish) ¿Cómo lo sabe?
(How did you know?)

MATILDE

(Imitating Ana's accent) ¿Cómo lo sabe?
(How did you know?)

   They laugh.

LANE

We've all met. You can leave now, Charles.

CHARLES

What happened to your wrist?

LANE

Can opener.

CHARLES

Oh.

   Charles examines the bandage on Lane's wrist.
   She pulls her hand away.

MATILDE

¿Ha usted estado alguna vez en Brasil?
(Have you ever been to Brazil?)

ANA

Una vez, para estudiar rocas.
(Once to study rocks.)

MATILDE

(For a moment not understanding the Spanish pronunciation) Rocas?
Ah, *rochas!*
(Ah, rocks! In Brazil it is pronounced "hochas.")

ANA

Sí! *rochas!* *(Pronounces it "hochas.")*

They laugh.

VIRGINIA

Should we sit down?

LANE

Virginia!

They all sit down.

(To Virginia) Could you get us something to drink.

VIRGINIA

What would you like?

MATILDE

I would like a coffee.

ANA

That sounds nice. I'll have coffee, too.

VIRGINIA

Charles?

CHARLES

Nothing for me, thanks.

VIRGINIA

Lane?

LANE

I would like some hard alcohol in a glass with ice. Thank you.

Virginia exits.

So.

CHARLES

Lane. I know this is unorthodox. But I want us to know each other.

ANA

You are very generous to have me in your home.

LANE

Not at all.

ANA

Yes, you are very generous. I wanted to meet you. I am not a home-wrecker. The last time I fell in love it was with my husband, a long time ago. He was a geologist and a very wild man, an alcoholic. But so fun! So crazy! He peed on lawns and did everything bad and I loved it. But I did not want to have children with him because he was too wild, too crazy. I said you have to stop drinking and then he did stop drinking and then he died of cancer when he was thirty-one.

Matilde murmurs with sympathy.

My heart was broken and I said to myself: I will never love again. And I didn't. I thought I was going to meet my husband in some kind of afterlife with fabulous rocks. Blue and green rocks. And then I met Charles. When Charles said he was married I said Charles we should stop but then Charles referred to Jewish law and I had to say that I agreed and that was that. I wanted you to understand.

LANE

Well, I don't understand. What about Jewish law.

CHARLES

In Jewish law you are legally obligated to break off relations with your wife or husband if you find what is called your *bashert*.

ANA

Your soul mate.

CHARLES

You are *obligated* to do this. Legally bound. There's something—metaphysically—objective about it.

LANE

You're not Jewish.

CHARLES

I know. But I heard about the *bashert*—on a radio program. And it always stuck with me. When I saw Ana I knew that was it. I knew she was my *bashert*.

ANA

There is a *midrash* that says when a baby is forty days old, inside the mother's stomach, God picks out its soul mate, and people have to spend the rest of their lives running around to find each other.

LANE

So you are Jewish?

ANA

Yes.

LANE

And your husband was a geologist.

ANA

Yes.

LANE

And you're from Argentina.

ANA

Yes.

LANE

Well. It's all making sense.

CHARLES

Lane. Something very objective happened to me. It's as though I suddenly tested positive for a genetic disease that I've had all along. *Ana has been in my genetic code.*

ANA

Yes. It is strange. We didn't feel guilty because it was so *objective*.

CHARLES

Lane. Something very objective happened to me. It's as though I suddenly tested positive for a genetic disease that I've had all along. *Ana has been in my genetic code.*

ANA

Yes. It is strange. We didn't feel guilty because it was so *objective*. And yet both of us are moral people. I don't know Charles very well but I think he is moral but to tell you the truth even if he were immoral I would love him because the love I feel for your husband is so overpowering.

LANE

And this is what you've come to tell me. That you're both innocent according to Jewish law.

ANA AND CHARLES

Yes.

Virginia enters with the drinks.

MATILDE

Thank you.

ANA

Thank you.

Lane takes a glass from Virginia.

LANE

(To Virginia) Charles has come to tell me that according to Jewish law, he has found his soul mate, and so our marriage is dissolved. He doesn't even need to feel guilty. How about that.

VIRGINIA

You have found your *bashert*.

LANE

How the hell do you know about a *bashert*?

VIRGINIA

I heard it on public radio.

CHARLES

I'm sorry that it happened to you, Lane. It could just as well have happened the other way. You might have met your *bashert*, and I would have been forced to make way. There are things—big invisible things—that come unannounced—they walk in, and we have to give way. I would even congratulate you. Because I have always loved you.

LANE

Well. Congratulations.

A silence. A cold one.

MATILDE

Would anyone like to hear a joke?

ANA

I would.

Matilde tells a short joke in Portuguese.
Ana laughs. No one else laughs.

¡Qué bueno! ¡Qué chiste más bueno!
(What a good joke!)

(To Lane) You are firing Matilde?

LANE

Yes.

ANA

Then we'll hire her to clean our house. I hate to clean. And Charles likes things to be clean. At least I think he does. Charles? Do you like things to be clean?

CHARLES

Sure. I like things to be clean.

ANA

Matilde? Would you like to work for us?

MATILDE

There is something you should know. I don't like to clean so much.

ANA

Of course you don't. Do you have any other skills?

MATILDE

I can tell jokes.

ANA

Perfect. She's coming to live with us.

LANE

My God! You can't just walk into my home and take everything away from me.

ANA

I thought you fired this young woman.

LANE

Yes. I did.

ANA

Have you changed your mind?

LANE

I don't know. Maybe.

ANA

Matilde, do you have a place to live?

MATILDE

No.

ANA

So she'll come live with us.

VIRGINIA

Matilde is like family.

MATILDE

What?

VIRGINIA

Matilde is like a sister to me.

ANA

Is this true?

MATILDE

I don't know. I never had a sister.

VIRGINIA

We clean together. We talk, and fold laundry, as women used to do. They would gather at the public fountains and wash their clothes and tell stories. Now we are alone in our separate houses and it is terrible.

ANA

So it is Virginia who wants you to stay. Not Lane.

LANE

We both want her to stay. We love *(An attempt at the Brazilian pro-nunciation)* Matilde.

ANA

Matilde?

MATILDE

I am confused.

LANE

I depend on Matilde. I couldn't stand to replace her. Matilde— are you unhappy here with us?

MATILDE

I—

LANE

Is it the money? You could have a raise.

ANA

Matilde—you should do as you wish. My house is easy to clean. I own hardly anything. I own one table, two chairs, a bed, one painting and I have a little fish whose water needs to be changed. I don't have rugs so there is no vacuuming. But you would have to do Charles' laundry. I will not be his washerwoman.

VIRGINIA

Excuse me. But I think that people who are in love—really in love—would like to clean up after each other. If I were in love with Charles I would enjoy folding his laundry.

Virginia looks at Charles.
Lane looks at Virginia.
Virginia looks at Lane.

ANA

Matilde—what do you think? If you stay with us, there is only one condition: you will have to tell one joke a day. I like to laugh.

VIRGINIA

Please don't leave us, Matilde.

MATILDE

I will split my time. Half with Lane and Virginia, half with Ana and Charles. How is that?

ANA

Lane?

LANE

Matilde is a free agent.

ANA

Of course she is.

CHARLES

Well.
That's settled.

LANE

Are you leaving now?

CHARLES

Do you want me to leave?

LANE

Yes.

CHARLES

Okay. Then we'll leave.
Ana and I are going apple picking this afternoon.
She's never been apple picking.
Would anyone like to join us?

MATILDE

I've never been apple picking

CHARLES

So Matilde will come. Virginia?

VIRGINIA

I love apple picking.

LANE

Virginia!

CHARLES

Lane?

LANE

You must be insane! Apple picking! My god! I'M SORRY! But—apple picking? This is not a foreign film! We don't have an *arrangement*! You don't even *like* foreign films! Maybe you'll pretend to like foreign films, for *Ana*, but I can tell you now, Ana, he doesn't like them! He doesn't like reading the subtitles! It gives him a headache!

CHARLES

Lane. I don't expect you to—understand this—immediately. But since this thing—has happened to me—I want to live life to the fullest. I know—what it must sound like. But it's different. I want to go apple picking. I want to go to Machu Picchu. You can be part of that. I want to share my happiness with you.

LANE

I don't want your happiness.

MATILDE

(To Ana) Es cómo una telenovela.
(It's like a soap opera.)

CHARLES

Lane—I—

LANE

What.

CHARLES

I hope that you'll forgive me one day.

LANE

Go pick some apples.
Good-bye.

CHARLES

Good-bye.

ANA

Good-bye.

MATILDE

Good-bye.

VIRGINIA

I'll stay.

Ana, Matilde and Charles exit.

LANE

I want to be alone.

VIRGINIA

No, you don't.

LANE

Yes, I do.

VIRGINIA

No, you don't.
Do you want—I don't know—a hot water bottle?

LANE

No, I don't want a hot water bottle, Virginia.

VIRGINIA

I just thought—

LANE

—That I'm nine years old with a cold?

VIRGINIA

I don't know what else to do.

A pause.

LANE

You know, actually, I think I'd like one. It sounds nice.

6. Ana's Balcony

Ana and Matilde are up on Ana's balcony.
It is high above the white living room.
It is a small perch, overlooking the sea,
with two chairs, and a fish bowl.
Through French doors,
one can enter or exit the balcony.
A room leading to the balcony is suggested but unseen.
Ana and Matilde are surrounded by apples.
The following dialogue may be spoken
in a combination of Portuguese and Spanish
and subtitled in English.
Underneath the balcony,
Lane is in her living room.
She lies down with a hot water bottle.
Ana polishes an apple.
Ana and Matilde look around at all of the apples.

ANA

We're never going to eat all of these damn apples.

MATILDE

But it's nice to have so many.
So many that it's *crazy* to have so many.
Because you can never eat them all.

ANA

Yes.

Ana picks out an apple and eats it.

MATILDE

I like the green ones.
Which ones do you like?

ANA

The yellow ones. They're sweeter.

MATILDE

We could take one bite of each, and if it's not a really, really good apple we can throw it into the sea.

ANA

Now you're talking like a North American.

MATILDE

It will be fun.

ANA

Okay.

*They start taking bites of each apple
and if they don't think it's a perfect apple they throw it into the sea.
The sea is also Lane's living room.
Lane sees the apples fall into her living room.
She looks at them.*

MATILDE

I made up eighty-four new jokes since I started working for you. I only made up one at the other house. It was a good one though. Sometimes you have to *suffer* for the really good ones.

ANA

Why don't you tell jokes for a job?

MATILDE

Someday.

Matilde throws an apple core into the living room.

ANA

Why someday? Why not now?

MATILDE

I'm looking for the perfect joke. But I am afraid if I found it, it would kill me.

ANA

Why?

MATILDE

My mother died laughing.

ANA

I'm sorry.

MATILDE

Thank you.
She was laughing at one of my father's jokes.

ANA

What was the joke?

MATILDE

I'll never know.
Let's not talk about sad things.

CHARLES

(From offstage) Ana!

ANA

We're on the balcony!

Matilde bites an apple.

MATILDE

Try this one.

ANA

Mmmm. Perfecta.

Charles rushes in wearing scrubs.
He goes to Ana and kisses her all over
and continues to kiss her all over.

We were just eating apples.

CHARLES

Aren't they delicious?

ANA

Here is the very best one.

Charles takes a bite of the best apple.

CHARLES

Divine!
Excuse me, Matilde.
I need to borrow this woman.

He kisses Ana.
He picks up Ana and carries her off into the bedroom.

MATILDE

Have fun.

ANA AND CHARLES

Thank you! We will!

They exit.
Matilde, to the audience:

MATILDE

The perfect joke happens by accident. Like a boil on your back-side that you pop. The perfect joke is the perfect music. You want to hear it only once in your life, and then, never again.

A subtitle projects: Matilde Tries to Think Up the Perfect Joke.
She looks out at the sea.
She thinks.

7. Matilde, Virginia and Lane

Virginia is cleaning. She is happy.
Lane, in pajamas, shuffles cards.
Lane shouts to Matilde who is on the balcony:

LANE

Matilde! Your deal.

Matilde leaves the balcony.

VIRGINIA

Lane—your couch is filthy. Wouldn't it be nice to have a fresh, clean slip-cover? I could sew you one.

LANE

That would be nice. It would give you a project.

Matilde enters.

Your deal.

Matilde sits.
Above them, on the balcony,
Ana and Charles dance a slow dance.

So.
Are you happy there? At the other house?

MATILDE

Yes.

LANE

What's her house like?

MATILDE

It's little. She has a balcony that overlooks the sea.

LANE

What's her furniture like?

MATILDE

A table from one place—a chair from another place. It doesn't go together. But it's nice.

LANE

What does she cook?

MATILDE

I'm not a spy!

LANE

I'm sorry.

They play cards.
On the balcony,
Charles and Ana finish their dance.
They exit, into the bedroom.
Lane puts down a card.

Do they seem like they are very much in love?

MATILDE

Yes.

LANE

How can you tell?

MATILDE

They stay in bed half the day. Charles doesn't go to work. He cancels half his patients. He wants to spend all his time with Ana.

LANE

Oh.

A pause.

MATILDE

Because Ana is dying again.

VIRGINIA

What?

MATILDE

Her disease came back.
She says she won't take any medicine.
She says it's poison.
He says: you have to go to the hospital!
And she says: I won't go to the hospital!
Then they really fight.
It's like a soap opera.
Charles yells and throws things at the wall.

LANE

Charles never yells.

MATILDE

Oh, he yells.
They broke all the condiments and spices yesterday.
There was this one yellow spice—
it got in their hair and on their faces
until they were all yellow.

A spice jar goes flying from the balcony.
A cloud of yellow spice lands in Lane's living room.

LANE

She won't go to the hospital?

MATILDE

No.
I might have to spend more time at the other house.
To help.

VIRGINIA

Poor Charles.

LANE

Poor Charles?
Poor Ana.
Poor me!
Poor sounds funny if you say it lots of times in a row: poor, poor, poor, poor, poor, poor, poor. Poor. Poor. Poor. Doesn't it sound funny?

VIRGINIA

Lane? Are you all right?

LANE

Oh, me? I'm fine.

8. Ana and Charles Try to Read One Another's Mind

Ana and Charles on the balcony.
Ana is dressed in a bathrobe.

CHARLES

Eight.

ANA

No, seven. You were very close.

CHARLES

I'll go again.

ANA

Okay.

CHARLES

Four.

ANA

Yes!

CHARLES

I knew it! I could see four apples. Now: colors.

ANA

Okay.

CHARLES

I'll start.

ANA

Red.

CHARLES

No.

ANA

Blue.

CHARLES

No.

ANA

I give up.

CHARLES

Purple. We have to concentrate harder. Like this. Ready? You go.

ANA

I'm tired.

CHARLES

Sorry. I'll stop.

ANA

Why all these guessing games?

CHARLES

You know Houdini?

ANA

The magician?

CHARLES

Yes. Houdini and his wife practiced reading each other's minds. So that—if one of them died—they'd be able to talk to each other—you know, after.

ANA

Did it work?

CHARLES

No.

ANA

Oh.

CHARLES

But I love you more than Houdini loved his wife. He was distracted—by his magic. I'm not distracted. Ana. Let's go to the hospital.

ANA

I told you.
No hospitals!

Charles is sad.

Charles, don't be sad.

CHARLES

Don't be sad! My God!

ANA

I can't take this.
I'm going for a swim.
Matilde!
Come look after Charles.
I'm going swimming.

Ana exits.
Charles looks out over the balcony,
watching Ana run out to the water.

CHARLES

Ana! Think of a country under the water! I'll guess it from the balcony!

MATILDE

She can't hear you.

Charles disrobes to his underwear.
He throws his clothes off the balcony.
They land in Lane's living room.

CHARLES

Excuse me, Matilde. I'm going for a swim.

MATILDE

I thought you can't swim.

CHARLES

I'll learn to swim.

Underneath the balcony, in Lane's living room,
Lane comes across Charles's sweater.
She breathes it in.
Charles leans over the balcony.

Ana! What's the country? I think it's a very small country! Is it Luxembourg? Ana!

He runs off.
Matilde looks out over the water.
A pause.
Matilde is startled.
Suddenly, with great clarity,
Matilde thinks up the perfect joke.

MATILDE

My God.
Oh no.
My God.
It's the perfect joke.
Am I dead?
No.

9. Lane and Virginia. Then Matilde.

Lane sits with Charles's sweater in her hands.
Virginia enters, vacuuming.

LANE

Stop it!

VIRGINIA

What?

LANE

Stop cleaning!

VIRGINIA

Why?

LANE

I DON'T WANT ANYTHING IN MY HOUSE TO BE CLEAN
EVER AGAIN! I WANT THERE TO BE DIRT AND PIGS IN THE
CORNER. MAYBE SOME COW MANURE SOME BIG DIRTY
SHITTY COWS AND SOME SHITTY COW SHIT LOTS OF IT
AND LOTS OF DIRTY FUCKING SOCKS—AND NONE OF
THEM MATCH—NONE OF THEM—BECAUSE YOU KNOW
WHAT—THAT IS HOW I FEEL.

Lane unplugs the vacuum.

VIRGINIA

Wow. I'm sorry.

LANE

And you know what? I will not let my house be a breeding ground
for your weird obsessive dirt fetish. I will not permit you to feel
like a better person just because you push dirt around all day on
my behalf.

VIRGINIA

I was just trying to help.

LANE

Well, it's not helping.

VIRGINIA

I wonder—when it was—that you became—such a bitch? Oh,
yes, I remember. Since the day you were born, you thought that
anyone with a *problem* had a defect of the will. You're wrong about
that. Some people have problems, real problems—

LANE

Yes. I see people with *real problems* all day long. At the hospital.

VIRGINIA

I think—there's a small part of me that's enjoyed watching your
life fall apart. To see you lose your composure—for once! I thought:
we can be real sisters who tell each other real things. But I was
wrong. Well, fine. I'm not picking up your dry cleaning anymore.
I'm going to get a job.

LANE

What job?

VIRGINIA

Any job!

LANE

What are you qualified to do at this point?

VIRGINIA

No wonder Charles left. You have no compassion.

LANE	VIRGINIA
I do so have compassion.	Ana is a woman with compassion.
I do so have compassion!	

VIRGINIA

Really. How so.

LANE

I traded my whole life to help people who are sick! What do you do?

Virginia and Lane breathe.
Virginia and Lane are in a state of silent animal warfare,
a brand of warfare particular to sisters.

I'm going to splash some water on my face.

VIRGINIA

Good.

Lane exits.
Virginia, alone.
On the balcony, Ana puts on a record—
an aria, most likely Italian.
Ana listens to opera on the balcony, looking out over the sea.
Virginia dumps a plant on the ground and the dirt spills onto the floor.
She realizes with some surprise that she enjoys this.
Virginia makes a giant operatic mess in the living room.
Matilde enters.

MATILDE

What are you doing?
Virginia?

VIRGINIA

I'M MAKING A MESS!

Virginia finishes making her operatic mess.
The aria ends.
Ana leaves the balcony.

MATILDE

You are okay?

VIRGINIA

Actually. I feel fabulous.

Matilde sits down.
Matilde puts her head in her arms.
Lane enters.

LANE

What the hell happened here?

VIRGINIA

I was mad. Sorry.

Virginia flicks a speck of dirt.
Lane looks at Matilde.

LANE

(To Virginia) What's wrong with her?

Virginia shrugs.

MATILDE

It's a mess.

VIRGINIA

I'll clean it up.

MATILDE

Not this—Ana, Charles—it's a mess.

LANE

Have they—fallen out of love?

MATILDE

No.

VIRGINIA

Is she very sick?

MATILDE

Yes.

LANE

Oh.

VIRGINIA

How terrible.

MATILDE

Yes.
And now Charles has gone away.

LANE

What?

MATILDE

(To Lane) To Alaska.

VIRGINIA

What?

MATILDE

(To Virginia) To Alaska.

LANE

But—why?

MATILDE

He says he's going to chop down a tree for Ana.

VIRGINIA

What?

MATILDE

A "you" tree.
He called it a you tree.

> *Matilde points: you.*

VIRGINIA

A you tree?

MATILDE

A you tree. He says he's going to invent a new "you medicine."

VIRGINIA

My God. He's gone crazy with love!

LANE

He's not crazy. It's a yew tree. *(Spelling it out)* Y-E-W. A Pacific yew tree. The bark was made into Taxol in 1967. It makes cancer cells clog up with microtubules so they're slower to grow and divide.

MATILDE

He said it was a special tree.

LANE

Yes. It is a special tree.

MATILDE

He wants to plant the tree in Ana's courtyard so she can smell the tree from her balcony.
She won't go to the hospital. So he said he would bring the hospital to her.

VIRGINIA

That's beautiful.

LANE

It's not beautiful, Virginia. There is a woman dying, alone, while Charles chops down a fucking tree.
How heroic.

VIRGINIA

Does she need a doctor?

MATILDE

Yes. But she won't go to the hospital.
So I thought I would ask.
Do you know any doctors who go to the house?

VIRGINIA

You mean house calls?

MATILDE

Yes, house calls.

Virginia and Matilde look at Lane.

LANE

Why are you looking at me?

They continue to look at Lane.

You want me to take care of my husband's soul mate.

VIRGINIA

Look at her as a patient. Not a person.
You can do that.

LANE

If she wanted to see a doctor, she'd go to the hospital. I am *not* going to her house. It would be totally inappropriate.

They look at Lane.
In the distance, Charles walks slowly across the stage dressed in a parka,
looking for his tree.
A great freezing wind.

1 0. Lane Makes a House Call to Her Husband's Soul Mate

On Ana's balcony.
Lane listens to Ana's heart with a stethoscope.

LANE

Breathe in.
Breathe in again.

Lane takes off her stethoscope.

Are you having any trouble breathing?

ANA

No. But sometimes it hurts when I breathe.

LANE

Where?

ANA

Here.

LANE

Do you have pain when you're at rest?

ANA

Yes.

LANE

Where?

ANA

In my spine.

LANE

Is the pain sharp, or dull?

ANA

Sharp.

LANE

Does it radiate?

ANA

Like light?

LANE

I mean—does it move from one place to another?

ANA

Yes. From here to there.

LANE

How's your appetite?

ANA

Not great.
You must hate me.

LANE

Look— I'm being a doctor right now. That's all.

Lane palpates Ana's spine.

Does that hurt?

ANA

It hurts already.

LANE

I can't know anything without doing tests.

ANA

I know.

LANE

And you won't go to the hospital.

ANA

No.

LANE

All right.

ANA

Do you think I'm crazy?

LANE

No.

A small pause.

ANA

Well. Can I get you anything to drink? I have some iced tea.

LANE

Sure. Thank you.

> *Ana exits.*
> *Lane looks out over the balcony at the water.*
> *Lane starts to weep.*
> *Ana enters with iced tea.*

ANA

Lane?

LANE

Oh God! I'm *not* going to cry in front of you.

ANA

It's okay. You can cry. You must hate me.

LANE

I don't hate you.

ANA

Why are you crying?

LANE

Okay! I hate you!
You—glow—with some kind of—thing—I can't *acquire* that—this—thing—sort of—glows off you—like a veil—in reverse—you're like *anyone's* soul mate—because you have that—thing—you have a balcony—I don't have a balcony—Charles looks at you—he glows, too—you're like two glowworms—he never looked at me like that.

ANA

Lane.

LANE

I looked at our wedding pictures to see—maybe—he looked at me that way—back then—and no—he didn't—he looked at me with *admiration*—I didn't know there was another way to be looked at—how could I know—I didn't know his face was capable of *doing that*—the way he looked at you—in my living room.

ANA

I'm sorry.

LANE

No you're not. If you were really sorry, you wouldn't have done it. We do as we please, and then we say we're sorry. But we're not sorry. We're just—uncomfortable—watching other people in pain.

Ana hands Lane an iced tea.

Thank you.

Lane drinks her iced tea.
They both look at the fish in the bowl.

What kind of fish is that?

ANA

A fighting fish.

LANE

How old is it?

ANA

Twelve.

LANE

That's old for a fish.

ANA

I keep expecting it to die. But it doesn't.

Lane taps on the bowl.
The fish wriggles.

How did you and Charles fall in love?

LANE

He didn't tell you?

ANA

No.

LANE

Oh. Well, we were in medical school together. We were anatomy partners. We fell in love over a dead body.

They look at each other.
Lane forgives Ana.

ANA

Want an apple?

LANE

Sure.

Ana gives Lane an apple.
Lane takes a bite and stops.

Did Charles pick this apple?

ANA

I don't know who picked it.

Lane eats the apple.

LANE

It's good.

In the distance,
Charles walks across the stage in a heavy parka.
He carries a pick axe.
On the balcony, it is snowing.

11. Lane Calls Virginia

Lane and Virginia on the telephone.

LANE

I saw Ana.

VIRGINIA

And?

LANE

She's coming to live with me.

VIRGINIA

What?

LANE

She can't be alone. She's too sick. I invited her.

VIRGINIA

That's generous. I'm impressed.

LANE

So will you be around—during the day—to help Matilde look
after her?

VIRGINIA

Oh, me? No. I got a job.

LANE

What?

VIRGINIA

I got a job.

LANE

Doing what?

VIRGINIA

I'm a checkout girl. At the grocery store.

LANE

You're not.

VIRGINIA

I am. I had my first day. I liked it. I liked using the cash register. I liked watching the vegetables go by on the conveyer belt. Purple, orange, red, green, yellow. My colleagues were nice. They helped me if my receipts got stuck in the machine. There was fellow feeling among the workers. Solidarity. And I liked it.

LANE

Wow.

VIRGINIA

So, I'm sorry. But I'll be too busy to help you.

Pause.

LANE

You made that story up.

VIRGINIA

Fine.

LANE

So you'll help me.

VIRGINIA

You want my help?

LANE

Yes.

VIRGINIA

Are you sure?

LANE

Yes.

VIRGINIA

Say: I want your help.

A small pause.

LANE

I want your help.

VIRGINIA

Then I'll help you.

12. Ana and Virginia. Then Matilde. Then Lane.

All of Ana's possessions have been moved into Lane's living room.
Ana's fish is in a bowl on the coffee table.
There are bags of apples on the carpet.
And luggage. With clothes spilling out of a bag.
Virginia is preparing a special tray of food for Ana.
Virginia listens to Ana.

ANA

People talk about *cancer* like it's this special thing you have a *relationship* with. And it becomes blood count, biopsy, chemotherapy, radiation, bone marrow, blah blah blah blah blah. As long as I live I want to retain my own language.

Mientras tengo vida, quiero procurar mantener mi proprio idioma.

No extra hospital words. I don't want a relationship with a disease. I want to have a relationship with death. That's important. But to have a relationship with a *disease*—that's some kind of bourgeois invention. And I hate it.

Virginia gives Ana the tray.

Thank you.

Ana eats a bite.

VIRGINIA

Do you like it?

ANA

It's delicious. What is it?

VIRGINIA

A casserole. No one makes casserole anymore. I thought it might be comforting.

ANA

What's in it?

VIRGINIA

Things you wouldn't want to know about.

ANA

Well, it's good.
Thank you for taking care of me, Virginia.

Virginia is moved.

What's wrong?

VIRGINIA

I'm not used to people thanking me.

Matilde enters, holding a telegram.
She hands it to Ana.

MATILDE

There is a telegram. From Charles.

In the distance, Charles appears
wearing a heavy parka.
Inside the living room, it snows.

CHARLES

Dear Ana. Stop.
Have cut down tree. Stop.
Cannot get on plane with tree. Stop.
Must learn to fly plane. Stop.
Wait for me. Stop.
Your beloved, Charles.

ANA

I want him to be a nurse and he wants to be an explorer.
Asi es la vida.
(That's life.)

Charles exits.
Lane enters.

LANE

Hi.

ANA

Hello!

An awkward moment.

VIRGINIA

Would anyone like ice cream? I made some ice cream.

MATILDE

You *made* it?

VIRGINIA

It was no trouble.

ANA

I love ice cream.

VIRGINIA

Do you like chocolate?

ANA

Who doesn't like chocolate. Crazy people.

VIRGINIA

I'll get spoons.

MATILDE

I'll help you.

> *Matilde and Virginia exit.*
> *Lane sees Ana's fish.*

LANE

He made it all right.

ANA

He's a strong fish.

> *Lane taps the fish bowl.*
> *The fish wriggles.*
> *Matilde and Virginia come back with spoons and ice cream.*
> *After a moment of hesitation, Lane takes a spoon from Virginia.*
> *They all eat ice cream out of the same container.*

Mmmm! Amazing!

MATILDE

It must be what God eats when he is tired.

ANA

So soft!

MATILDE

Sometimes ice cream in this country is so hard.

ANA

Sí.

LANE

I like ice cream.

They all eat ice cream.

ANA

Can you imagine a time before ice cream? When they couldn't keep things frozen? There was once a ship filled with ice—it sailed from Europe to South America. The ice melted by the time it got to South America. And the captain of the ship was bankrupt. All he had to sell when he got there was water.

VIRGINIA

A ship full of water.

MATILDE

A ship full of water.

They finish the ice cream.
No one cleans up.

VIRGINIA

(To Ana) You look feverish. Are you warm?

ANA

I'm cold.

VIRGINIA

I'll get a thermometer.

ANA

No thermometers!

LANE

How about a blanket?

ANA

Okay. I'd like a blanket.

LANE

(To Virginia) Where do I keep blankets?

VIRGINIA

I'll show you.

Lane and Virginia exit.

ANA

Matilde. My bones hurt.

MATILDE

I know they do.

ANA

Do you know what it feels like when your bones hurt?

MATILDE

No.

ANA

I hope you never know.
Matilde. You once told me that your father killed your mother
with a joke.

MATILDE

Yes.

ANA

I would like you to kill me with a joke.

MATILDE

I don't want to kill you.
I like you.

ANA

If you like me, help me.

MATILDE

What about Charles? Will you wait for him?

ANA

No.

MATILDE

Why?

ANA

I'd lose all my bravery.

MATILDE

I understand.

ANA

You'll do it then?

A pause.

MATILDE

Okay.

ANA

When?

MATILDE

When you want me to.

ANA

You don't need time to make up a joke?.

MATILDE

I made it up on your balcony.

ANA

Tomorrow, then.

MATILDE

Tomorrow.

Lane enters with a blanket.
She hands it to Ana.

LANE

I hope it's warm enough.

ANA

Thank you.
(To Matilde) Good night.

MATILDE

(To Ana) Good night.

Ana puts her head on the pillow, closing her eyes.

(Whispering to Lane) Are you coming?

LANE

In a minute.

Matilde exits.
Lane sits on the floor and watches Ana sleep.
She guards her the way a dog would guard a rival dog,
if her rival were sick.

13. Matilde Tells Ana a Joke

The light turns from night to day.
The next day.
Lane, Virginia and Matilde are gathered around Ana.

ANA

I want to say good-bye to everyone before Matilde tells me a joke.

LANE

Can't I give you anything for the pain?

ANA

No.

LANE

You're sure?

ANA

Yes. Good-bye, Lane.

LANE

Good-bye, Ana.

They embrace.

ANA

Take care of Charles.

LANE

You think I'll be taking care of him?

ANA

Of course.

LANE

Why?

ANA

You love him.
Good-bye Virginia.

Virginia weeps.

Don't cry. Thank you for taking care of me.

Virginia weeps.

Oh—see? That makes it worse. Oh, Virginia. I can't take it.
Matilde. Let's have the joke.

MATILDE

Are you ready?

ANA

Yes.
Everyone's always dying lying down.
I want to die standing up.

Ana stands.

(To Lane and Virginia) The two of you had better leave the room.
I don't want you dying before your time.

They nod.
They leave.

Matilde.
Deseo el chiste ahora.
(I want the joke now.)

The lights change.
Music.
Matilde whispers a joke in Ana's ear.
We don't hear it.

We hear sublime music instead.
A subtitle projects: The Funniest Joke in the World.
Ana laughs and laughs.
Ana collapses.
Matilde kneels beside her.
Matilde wails.

MATILDE

Ohhh . . .

Lane and Virginia rush in.
Lane checks Ana's pulse.
The women look at one another.

VIRGINIA

What do we do?

LANE

I don't know.

VIRGINIA

You're the doctor!

LANE

I've never seen someone die in a house before.
Only in a hospital.
Where they clean everything up.

VIRGINIA

What do the nurses do?

MATILDE

They close the eyes.

LANE

That's right.

Matilde closes Ana's eyes.

MATILDE

And they wash the body.

LANE

I'll wash her.

Lane goes to get a towel and a bowl of water.

VIRGINIA

Should we say a prayer?

MATILDE

You say a prayer, Virginia.
A prayer cleans the air the way water cleans the dirt.

VIRGINIA

Ana. I hope you are apple picking.

Lane enters with a bowl of water.
She washes Ana's body.
Time slows down.

CHARLES

(From offstage) Ana!

Charles pounds on the door.

Ana! Ana!

The women look at one another.
Lane goes to Charles.
Charles walks in carrying an enormous tree.
He is sweating and breathing heavily.
He has carried his tree great distances.

I brought back this tree.
The bark—

LANE

I know.

CHARLES

It won't help?

LANE

No.

CHARLES

Why?

LANE

Charles.

CHARLES

You were here?

LANE

Yes.

CHARLES

Can I see her?

> *Lane nods.*

LANE

Charles?

> *Lane kisses Charles on the forehead.*

CHARLES

Thank you. Will you hold my tree?

> *Lane nods.*
> *Lane holds the tree.*
> *Charles moves toward Ana's body.*

He collapses over her body
as the lights come up on Matilde.

14. Matilde

Matilde, to the audience:

MATILDE

This is how I imagine my parents.

Ana and Charles transform into Matilde's mother and father.
Under Charles's parka he is dressed as Matilde's father.
Under Ana's bathrobe, she is dressed as Matilde's mother.

My mother is about to give birth to me.
The hospital is too far away.
My mother runs up a hill in December and says: now!
My mother is lying down under a tree.
My father is telling her a joke to try and keep her calm.

Matilde's father whispers a joke in Portuguese to Matilde's mother.

My mother laughed.
She laughed so hard that I popped out.
My mother said I was the only baby who laughed
when I came into the world.
She said I was laughing at my father's joke.
I laughed to take in the air.
I took in some air, and then I cried.

Matilde looks at her parents.
A moment of completion between them.
Matilde looks at the audience.

I think maybe heaven is a sea of untranslatable jokes.
Only everyone is laughing.

THE END

A Note on Subtitles

The director might consider projecting subtitles in the play for some scene titles and some stage directions. I suggest these:

A woman tells a joke in Portuguese. (page 9)

Lane. (9)

Virginia. (10)

Matilde. (11)

Virginia takes stock of her sister's dust. (19)

Lane and Virginia experience a primal moment during which they are seven and nine years old. (30)

Matilde tries to think up the perfect joke. (31)

Matilde tries to think up the perfect joke. (33)

Virginia has a deep impulse to order the universe. (37)

Charles performs surgery on the woman he loves. (51)

Ana. (52)

Charles. (53)

They fall in love. (55)

They fall in love some more. (55)

They fall in love completely. (55)

Ana's balcony. (70)

Matilde tries to think up the perfect joke. (74)

Ana and Charles try to read one another's mind. (77)

Lane makes a house call to her husband's soul mate. (88)

Lane forgives Ana. (93)

Lane calls Virginia. (94)

The funniest joke in the world. (106)

A Note on Jokes

Thanks is due to all the people who helped me with jokes and translations in *The Clean House*: Caridad Svich, Fernando Oliveira, Anna Fluck, Giovanna Sardelli, Claudine Barros.

I want the choice of jokes to be somewhat open, allowing for the possibility that different productions may come up with different and more perfect Brazilian jokes. So please use these jokes as you will.

Joke #1, to be told in Act 1, Scene 1:

Um homem tava a ponto de casar e ele tava muito nervosa ao preparar-se pra noite de nupias porque ele nunca tuvo sexo en la vida de ele. Enton ele vai pra médico e pergunta: "O que que eu devo fazor?" O médico fala: "Não se preocupa. Voce coloca uma nota de dez dolares na bolso direito y voce practica: '10, 10, 10, 10.'"

Enton el homen vai pra casa y practica todo semana: "10,10,10." Aí ele volta pra médico y lhe fala: "Muito bem! Agora você coloca uma nota de, 10 no bolso direito e uma nota do 20 (vinte) no bolso esquerdo e practica: '10, 20; 10, 20; 10, 20; 10 20.'"

Ele foi pra casa praticou toda semana: "10, 20; 10, 20; 10, 20." Ele volta pra medico y ele falou: "É isso aí! Agora você coloca uma nota de 10 no bolso direito, uma de 20 no bolso esquerdo e uma de 100 (cem) na frente. Aí você practica: '10, 20, 100; 10, 20, 100; 10, 20, 100.'"

Aí ele casou. A noite de núpcias chegou. Ele tava con sua mulher todo bonita e gustosa e ele comencou a fazer amor: "10, 20, 100; 10, 20, 100; 10, 20, 100. Ai, que se foda o trocado: 100, 100, 100!!!"

TRANSLATION:

A man is getting married. He's never had sex and he's very nervous about his wedding night. So, he goes to a doctor and he says, "I'm really nervous, what should I do?" The doctor says, "Don't worry about it. Go home and put a ten-dollar bill in your right pocket and you practice: '10! 10! 10!,' moving your hips to the left."

So, he goes home and after a week of practice, he returns to the doctor who says, "Very good. Now, go back home and put a ten-dollar bill in your right-hand pocket, a twenty-dollar bill in your left-hand pocket and go: '10! 20! 10! 20!'" *(The joke teller moves hips from side to side)*
So, he practices, does very well, returns to the doctor who says, "Perfect! Now you're going to put a ten-dollar bill in your left-hand pocket, a twenty-dollar bill in your right-hand pocket and a hundred-dollar dollar bill in front, where you will go like this, '10! 20! 100!, 10! 20!, 100!'"
The man practices as he is told, goes back to the doctor who says, "Perfect! You're ready to go!"
The big day arrives and the man is very excited about his night with his wife. The time comes and he is in bed and he starts with his wife: "10! 20! 100!, 10! 20! 100!, 10! 20! 100! Oh, fuck the change: 100! 100! 100!"

Joke #2, to be told in Act 1, Scene 14:

Por que os homens na cama são como comida de microondas.
Estão prontos em trinta segundos.

TRANSLATION:

Why are men in bed like microwave food?
They're done in thirty seconds.

Joke #3, to be told in Act 2, Scene 5:

O melhor investimento que existe é comprar um argentino pelo valor que ele vale e depois vendê-lo pelo valor que ele acha que vale.

TRANSLATION:

The best investment ever is to buy an Argentinean for what he is really worth and later sell him for what he thinks he is worth.

A NOTE ON ACT 2, SCENE 6

If the actors playing Ana and Matilde can speak a combination of Spanish and Portuguese, I suggest using this combination of Spanish, Portuguese and English (subtitled where necessary) for this section of the scene.

ANA

Nunca podremos comer todas estas malditas manzanas.
(We're never going to eat all of these damn apples.)

MATILDE

Mas é muito bom ter muitas . . .
É uma loucura ter tantas
Porque nos nunca vamos poder comer todas.
(But it's nice to have so many . . .
So many that it's crazy to have so many
Because you can never eat them all.)

ANA

Es así!
(Yes!)

    Ana picks out an apple and eats it.

MATILDE

Eu gosto das maçãs verdes.
De qual que você gosta?
(I like the green ones.
Which ones do you like?)

ANA

Las amarillas, son las mas dulces.
(The yellow ones. They're sweeter.)

MATILDE

A gente pode dar uma mordida em cada uma e se a maca não for real-
mente divina a gente joga no mar.
(We could take a bite of each apple and if it's not a really, really good apple we
can throw it into the sea.)

ANA

Ché! Hablás como Norte Americana.
(Now you're talking like a North American.)

MATILDE

Sería bem divertido.

(It will be fun.)

ANA

Okay.

> *They start taking bites of each apple*
> *and if they don't think it's a perfect apple*
> *they throw it into the sea.*
> *The sea is also Lane's living room.*
> *Lane sees the apples fall into her living room.*
> *She looks at them.*

MATILDE

I made up eighty-four new jokes since I started working for you. I only made up one at the other house. It was a good one though. Sometimes you have to *suffer* for the really good ones.

ANA

Why don't you tell jokes for a job?

MATILDE

Someday.

> *Matilde throws an apple core into the living room.*

ANA

Why someday? Why not now?

MATILDE

I'm looking for the perfect joke. But I am afraid if I found it, it would kill me.

ANA

Por que?
(Why?)

MATILDE

Minha mãe morreu dando risada.
(My mother died laughing.)

ANA

Lo siento.
(I'm sorry.)

MATILDE

Obrigada.
Ela estava rindo de uma das piadas do meu pai.
(Thank you.
She was laughing at one of my father's jokes.)

ANA

Cuál era el chiste?
(What was the joke?)

MATILDE

Eu nunca saberei. Mas não vamos falar de coisas tristes.
(I'll never know.
Let's not talk about sad things.)

CHARLES

(From offstage) Ana!

    Matilde bites an apple.

Try this one.

ANA

Mmmm. Perfecta!

    The scene continues as is . . .

Late

a cowboy song

*This play is for all the lady cowboys of heart and mind
who ride outside the city limits of convention.
Special thanks to Paula and Anne.
And Peggy Munson.*

PRODUCTION HISTORY

Late: a cowboy song was produced at The Ohio Theatre in New York City, by Clubbed Thumb (Arne Jokela, Meg MacCary, Maria Striar and Jay Worthington, producers) on April 21, 2003. The production was directed by Debbie Saivetz; the set design was by Andromache Chalfant, the lighting design was by Steve O'Shea, the costume design was by Eric Hall, the sound design was by Bray Poor and original music was composed by Michael Escamilla; the stage manager was Erin Cameron. The cast was as follows:

CRICK	Mather Zickel
MARY	Carla Harting
RED	Addie Johnson

CHARACTERS

CRICK: Charming, fragile and childlike.

MARY: Keeps her journal locked.

RED: She's no cowgirl, she's a cowboy.

Note: Red talks slow. Crick talks fast. Mary's somewhere in the middle. Crick, Mary, and Red need not be any particular race or ethnicity.

PLACE

A version of Pittsburgh.
A silhouette of a messy kitchen.
An image of the Marlboro Man hovers in the distance,
against blue light.

NOTES ON PRODUCTION

Blue, the horse, and the painting should be suggested or abstracted. For example, in the Clubbed Thumb production, the horse was simply a wooden saddle stand, complete with stirrups, lit beautifully. The painting was an empty frame. Blue was invisible. Having said that, I would not say no to a real horse.

The hyperrealism of a messy kitchen should float up against the sensation of a deep, abstracted landscape—horizon lines, empty space. Reds, blues, greens—think of Rothko. Think of Crick's obsession with modernism, up against Mary's obsession with open land.

Transitions should be fluid, without blackouts

SPECIAL THANKS

I am indebted to Anne Fausto-Sterling and her groundbreaking book, *Sexing the Body* (Basic Books, 2000).

THE MUSIC

It would be nice if the actress playing Red could play the guitar. At the very least, she should be able to sing, accompanied by a live guitar. When Red sings, she ought to have a real cowboy outfit. Don't forget the chaps. The lyrics of the songs are mine. The music is up to you. Michael Escamilla wrote beautiful music for the Clubbed Thumb production (for information, contact Fifi Oscard Agency, Inc., Francis Del Duca, 110 West 40th Street, 16th Floor, New York, NY 10018). Think simple, iconic melodies. Yodling is optional. Some melodies should feel more honky-tonk. Others— more like prayer under the night sky.

Part 1

||╚╝|||

1. You're Late

A man—Crick—sits among dirty dishes.
A woman—Mary—steps in the door.

CRICK

You're late.

MARY

I know, I'm sorry.

CRICK

Where were you?

MARY

I ran into an old friend on the street.

CRICK

There's some food on the stove.

MARY

You cooked! Thanks.

CRICK

I love you, sugarplum.

They kiss.

MARY

I love you, too. Smells good. What is it?

CRICK

Beef. Who'd you run into?

MARY

That girl we went to school with who always wore a money clip instead of carrying a purse.

CRICK

Oh, her. What's her name?

MARY

I haven't seen her in years.

CRICK

I didn't know you and her were friends.

MARY

Red. Red is her name.

CRICK

That's right. Red.

MARY

What's wrong with Red? I like her.

CRICK

She used to make jokes all the time that weren't funny.

MARY

I think she's funny.

CRICK

Maybe I have a better sense of humor than you do.
Just kidding.
What did you do with—"Red"?

MARY

Had some coffee.

CRICK

Where?

MARY

What does it matter?

CRICK

I want to be able to imagine your day—every moment—like a
beautiful detailed painting—the sort a Russian might paint on a
hollow egg.

MARY

I don't think any Russians are interested in painting my life.

CRICK

Where'd you get coffee?

MARY

Green Shutters.

CRICK

You took her *there*?

MARY

What's wrong with Green Shutters?

CRICK

You got coffee at a Chinese restaurant?

MARY

There are no other restaurants on that block.

CRICK

That's where *we* go.

MARY

I told you—there are no other restaurants—

CRICK

You were supposed to be home for dinner.

MARY

I know. I'm sorry. I should have called. Thanks for cooking.

She begins to eat her food.

CRICK

I have a headache.

MARY

Oh—you do? I'm sorry. The one you get right there?

CRICK

Yes.

MARY

Do you want me to rub your head?

CRICK

Sure. Thanks.

She starts rubbing his head.

Do you have any money?

MARY

Why?

CRICK

Can't you just answer the question—simply and elegantly—yes
or no—in the same manner in which it was asked?

MARY

I have a little money.

CRICK

Can I have some?

MARY

What for?

CRICK

I just need it. Do you not trust me?

MARY

Of course I trust you.

She stops rubbing his head.

CRICK

Aw—why'd you stop?

MARY

Sorry.

CRICK

So you'll give me the money.

MARY

I just want to know what it's for.

CRICK

It's a surprise.

MARY

How much?

CRICK

Five hundred dollars.

MARY

Jesus.

CRICK

You don't have five hundred dollars? I thought you were an heiress.

MARY

I'm not an heiress.

CRICK

You're more of an heiress than me.

MARY

That's true. Most people are more of an heiress than you. They—like—inherit money from their jobs. Like a paycheck.

CRICK

Look—fuck you.

MARY

I don't like your language.

CRICK

In a just society people with more money give money to people with less money. I know you agree with that.

MARY

Yes—I do.

CRICK

If I had more money than you I'd give my money to you.

MARY

But you never do have more money than me.

CRICK

But I could.

MARY

Yes. You could. But you don't.

CRICK

You want to tally it up? See who's spent more on who? In the mind
of God, who do you think has spent more money on who? Me or
you?

MARY

Me.

CRICK

You think God cares? It's just money. It's not your soul. Money is
meant to be spent.

MARY

Right.

CRICK

And I know you have five hundred dollars. Just sitting there.
Doing nothing. Your soul should just sit there. Doing nothing. Not
your money.

MARY

I'll write you a check.

CRICK

Thanks.

MARY

It's my whole savings.

CRICK

Don't worry, honey. I'll give it back to you.
I'm just going to borrow it.
How is whatsherface, anyway?

MARY

Red?

CRICK

Yeah, Red. What kind of name is Red, anyway. Who does she think she is, the Marlboro Man?

MARY

She is, kind of. Red's a cowboy.

CRICK

Oh, yeah right—a cowboy in Pittsburgh.

MARY

She is—she wears a cowboy hat. She wore a big hat into the Green Shutters. It was kind of funny. People looked at her and she just tipped her hat. She does things to saddles and harnesses. She rides things. She can make a horse fall asleep—she sings horse lullabies for a job. She gets paid for it. She says it's beautiful, when a horse falls asleep. She says it's like if God fell asleep. Because God would sleep standing up—just in case he had to wake up—to take care of anything.

CRICK

It's cows that fall asleep standing up. Not horses.

MARY

Oh—I thought she said horses.

CRICK

Cows. Horses only fall asleep if they have to—if they're put in stalls. They should roam free. Don't you think?

MARY

It's nicer to think of horses falling asleep. I don't like to think of a cow falling asleep. It's not as pretty. Why is a cow not as pretty as a horse?

CRICK

People in India think cows are beautiful. They put cows in their art.

MARY

I don't know about that.

CRICK

What'd you talk about—you and *Red*?

MARY

I told you—horses falling asleep.

CRICK

Did she make a pass at you?

MARY

Yeah—I fucked her.
No, she didn't make a pass at me.
Jesus.

CRICK

What's wrong with you? Using language like that?

MARY

I'm going to my mother's house.

CRICK

You haven't eaten your dinner.

MARY

I'm not hungry.

CRICK

Why not? Hey—did you eat *dinner* with her at the Green Shutters?

MARY

No.

CRICK

The coffee—filled you up—all by itself?

MARY

Yes.

CRICK

Never known you to be satisfied by cream and sugar.

MARY

I didn't have cream or sugar in my coffee.

CRICK

Oh, you took it cowboy style. That's your new way, huh, tough girl?

MARY

Yeah. That's right. I don't like your tone of voice. I'm going to see my mother.

CRICK

You didn't finish your dinner.

MARY

I'll eat it later. I want to see my mother.

CRICK

Tell her I say hello.

MARY

I will.

Mary turns to go.

CRICK

Bye.

Crick looks pained.
Mary turns back.

MARY

I'm sorry.

CRICK

What for?

MARY

For being late.

CRICK

Don't go to your mother's. Stay here with me. We'll make up.

MARY

What do you mean: we'll make up?

CRICK

You know what I mean. We'll make up. Come here.

Crick pulls Mary to him.
They kiss.

2 . Red

A woman—Red—in a cowboy hat—
leans against a tree and strums a cowboy tune on her guitar.
Stars and moon overhead.
She sings:

RED

Oh, as the sun sets
The horses do sleep
The fields they are long
And the crick it is deep . . .

Oh, find me a child
Who grows into a man
Who cries like a bird
And flies like a—crayon . . .

3. Summer

CRICK

You're late?

MARY

Yes.

CRICK

How late?

MARY

I think—I don't know—I wasn't keeping records . . .

CRICK

Don't you just know these things?

MARY

You're supposed to keep records. I used to keep records in my diary—I put a red mark—but I forgot.

CRICK

Mary.

MARY

Once when I was little—

CRICK

Should we take a test?

MARY

I don't want to. I'm scared of those tests.

CRICK

So we'll just wait and see.

MARY

I guess.

CRICK

What about when you were little?

MARY

I forget.

CRICK

(Overlapping with Mary below) Well, you know how I feel about it.

MARY

Oh, I remember. When I was little I put a red mark in my diary to keep track and someone saw my diary and asked what's that red mark for and I had to say that's when I have my period.
And they passed my diary around the cafeteria.

CRICK

Oh, honey. That's horrible.

He kisses her on her forehead.

No wonder you don't want to keep track.

MARY

I'm glad I'm grown-up now.

She thinks about being grown-up and starts to cry.

CRICK

Aw honey, aw honey, aw honey, don't cry. It'll work out. We'll get married.

MARY

Oh, Crick.

CRICK

What kind of wedding do you want to have?

MARY

I don't know.

CRICK

Would you have bridesmaids?

MARY

Oh—I don't know—

CRICK

I think we shouldn't have bridesmaids. Those matching dresses—
it's weird. Like seven nurses in lilac preparing to take you to your
deathbed. I don't want to have a big party. Something small.
Because it's between us, right?

MARY

Yes.

CRICK

It's about our love. I don't want people getting drunk and falling
all over a dance floor. That's no way to celebrate our love.

MARY

You're right. I never thought of that.

CRICK

A lot of poetry and music and flowers. Love isn't pretty like that.
They try to make it pretty. Like a funeral. Cover up what's really
going on. With people in uniforms running around arranging things.
And meat cooked all wrong. Love is between two people. It's not
about acquaintances throwing up in the bathroom. I hate that.

MARY

I want *some* flowers at the wedding.

CRICK

You do? Aw, honey. What kind of flowers do you want?

MARY

Those little blue ones, like you find in a field.

CRICK

We'll have lots of those flowers, lots and lots and lots.

MARY

I think they're called forget-me-nots.

CRICK

I love it when you know stuff about plants.

We'll have forget-me-nots. A whole bundle. You'll carry some, I'll carry some. No music, okay? But we'll have a whole room of those little blue flowers. And some really good meat, cooked over a grill. We should get married soon.

MARY

Aw, Crick.

CRICK

Before you start to—show.

MARY

Oh—

CRICK

What do you want to name our kid?

MARY

I was thinking Jack?

CRICK

I never liked the name Jack.

Pause.
Mary looks pained.

What's wrong?

MARY

I love the name Jack.
All my dead relations are named Jack.

CRICK

Oh, that's right. I'm sorry, honey.
Jack, it is. What do I care about a name! We're gonna have a baby!

Crick whirls Mary around the room.

But it has to have my last name, okay?

MARY

Why?

CRICK

There're only three Thorndiggers left in the United States. Plenty
of Smiths, no offense honey.

MARY

Maybe Smith could be the middle name.

A pause.

Crick? Maybe Smith could be the middle name.

CRICK

Hold on. I'm thinking. Jack Smith Thorndigger.

MARY

Jack Smith Thorndigger.

CRICK

Sounds like we're trying to belong to a country club, having a last
name for a middle name. But if it's what you want—okay—I like
it. I like it.

MARY

What'd you do with that five hundred dollars?

CRICK

It's a surprise.
I'm so happy. Are you happy?

MARY

Yes.

CRICK

You've made me the happiest man in the world, Mrs. Thorndigger. I hope we have a boy, don't you? If we have a girl and she
wears those lavender miniskirts and the boys chase her around
I wouldn't be able to stand it. I'd have to follow her all around, to
school and to parties, just to make sure boys weren't looking at
her funny.

MARY

Hey—

CRICK

What?

MARY

You never asked me to marry you.

CRICK

Aw, honey.

MARY

I want you to ask.

He gets down on his knees.

CRICK

With eyes the size of tulips, and the most perfect nose in Pennsylvania, Mary Smith: we have loved each other since we were
eight years old. Will you marry me?

MARY

Yes, I'll marry you—my dearest love.

CRICK

My beautiful Mary Thorndigger. I love you.

MARY

I love you, too.

> *They kiss.*
> *Crick buries his head in Mary's lap.*

Honey—there's one thing.

CRICK

What is it darling?

MARY

If we have a baby, you gotta get a job.

CRICK

No problem. I'll get a job.

4. Crick Gets a Job

At the museum. A job interview.

CRICK

Because I've always wanted to be a museum guard.
Because I've always loved paintings.
Because I've always thought that paintings should be in a person's house and not in a museum.
Don't get me wrong. I *do* want paintings to be in a museum.
And I swear to protect them. I would never remove one.
Or touch one.
I promise to guard them and uphold all the regulations.
I've always wanted to be a museum guard. My whole life long.
Because how could you really look at a painting and love it and understand it if you see it for five minutes—you've got to look at

it the whole day long. Maybe for your whole life long.
I'll be the best museum guard you've ever seen. I will.
I'm going to have a baby. I'm going to be the best father
and the best museum guard you've ever seen.

A pause while the museum interviewer asks: why's your name Crick?

Oh, yeah, people are always asking me that.
My father named me after the creek I was conceived near.
Sort of a funny name, I know.
I always wished I were named John or Mark or something like that.
My wife and I won't make the same mistake with our baby.
We're naming it Jill, if it's a girl.
My wife—she wanted to name it Blue—but I said no honey—the
kids at school will make fun of it. Our child should have a nice old-
fashioned name out of the Bible like Jill.

A pause while the museum interviewer speaks.

Oh? Really? Maybe it's the translation I read.

A pause while the museum interviewer speaks.

Really? I do. Well, that's wonderful. Thank you. I can't wait to start.

5. At the Green Shutters

Red wears a cowboy hat. Mary looks pregnant.
Mary and Red, finishing a large bowl of soup for two people.
Two fortune cookies on the table.

MARY

I love this soup. I'm going to learn to make it at home. The clear
soup—with vegetables—all bright and clear and separate in the
broth. You know how in Campbell's soup the vegetables get all
mushed together?

RED

Yeah.

MARY

I like it when the vegetables are separate. So a carrot really looks like a carrot. I wonder how they do that. I'm going to learn to make it at home.

RED

You know—I hear there's even better Chinese food outside of Pittsburgh.

MARY

Where?

RED

Places like New York. San Francisco.

MARY

Oh! Have you been there?

RED

Nope. You know me—can't bring a horse into the city.

MARY

No.

RED

But I hear they have the best Chinese food there. And not just Chinese food. But Asian food more generally.

MARY

What do you mean?

RED

The cuisine of other countries in Asia. Not just China.

MARY

Oh!

RED

Vietnamese, Japanese, Korean . . .

MARY

What's the food from Vietnam like?

RED

Never had it.

MARY

Me neither. I bet there's a cookbook. Or show on TV.

RED

They have everything on TV.

MARY

Yeah.
I wonder if they feel bad, making food for us in America.

RED

Who?

MARY

The Vietnamese and the Koreans. After those wars. Why would
they want to cook food for us, d'you think?

RED

Maybe they don't want to. Maybe it's for the money.

MARY

What exactly happened in those wars anyway? Who was fighting
who?

RED

The north, the south. It's always the north and the south.

MARY

Maybe if people appreciated—*really* appreciated—the cuisines of
other nations—they would say to themselves—my body has been
nourished by this other country. I will be good to its citizens.

RED

Could be.

MARY

Well, I just don't know.

RED

About wars? How they begin and how they end?

MARY

Yeah.

RED

Me neither.

MARY

I wish I knew.

RED

Me, too.
All I know is what a cowboy needs. Simple food. No fancy spices.

MARY

Sounds nice.

RED

See——I don't cook for other people. I cook for me.
One soul, eating under the night sky.

MARY

Can a soul eat?

RED

I reckon so.

MARY

Me, too.

A pause.

Well. We'd better have our fortune cookies. What time is it?

RED

I have no idea.

Mary looks at a clock.

MARY

I'm late.
That's all right.
You can't rush a fortune cookie.
It's—a ritual.

Mary opens her fortune cookie. She reads it. She is troubled.

Huh.

RED

What's wrong?

MARY

I keep getting the same fortune.

RED

What's that?

MARY

It says: your onion is someone else's water lily.

RED

What does that mean?

MARY

I don't know.

RED

You eat lots of onions?

MARY

Not many.

RED

Huh.

I hear sometimes pregnant ladies get a taste for onions.

MARY

No, not me. I don't know. Onions make you cry, I guess.
Maybe Crick is my onion. And he'd be someone else's water lily.

RED

He ever hit you?

MARY

My husband?

RED

Yeah.

MARY

No.
Of course not.
He's so gentle, he wouldn't hurt a fly. Why do you ask?

RED

Because sometimes you talk about him—like you're afraid of him.

MARY

Afraid of Crick? Nah. That's silly.

RED

What's he make you cry about?

MARY

Oh, I don't know. Stuff. What's your fortune?

RED

Your smile is so lovely it makes everyone realize that the world is
a beautiful place.

MARY

It's true.

RED

Aw.

A pause. They look at each other.

So you got a name for the baby yet?

MARY

I want to name her—Blue—if it's a girl. I feel like it's a girl.

RED

That's a pretty name. Blue.

MARY

It's kind of after you.

RED

Really?

MARY

Yeah—after I ran into you—I thought about your name. I thought, I want this baby to be a real individual-type person. Like Red is. So I thought I'd call her Blue.

RED

I'm flattered.

MARY

I hope you don't think that's weird. I mean, I know we don't know each other very well and all.

RED

No—no—I'm flattered.
Maybe I'll baby-sit for her—it—the baby—sometimes. When it gets born.

MARY

Maybe. I don't know. Crick says he wants it to be just me, him, and the baby. He likes the family intimacy feeling. With the lamps all aglow. Like Swedish paintings, he says.

RED

I never seen a Swedish painting.

MARY

Me neither. Crick goes to museums.

RED

Maybe we'll take it for walks.

MARY

What?

RED

The baby.

MARY

Oh—yes. The baby!

RED

I could show it the stables, outside the city limits.

MARY

Oh! That sounds like heaven.

6. Red Sings a Song

RED

Eatin' soup under the Pittsburgh sky
Eatin' soup looking in her eyes
Who am I to describe such fragile* delights
I'm a cowboy from Pennsylvania.

Sharin' our fortunes and sharin' rice
Sharin' one table and sharin' one night
Who am I to describe such fragile* delights
I'm a cowboy from Pennsylvania.

*Fragile is pronounced with a long "i."

7. Christmas Morning

Christmas music.
Crick rips open brown wrapping paper on a painting.
Crick and Mary see an abstract expressionist painting—
we see only a frame.
Crick leans it against the wall, reverent.
Crick and Mary look at the painting.

MARY

It's nice.

CRICK

Is that all?

MARY

How much was it?

CRICK

Never mind about that. Do you like it?

MARY

What do I do with it?

CRICK

What do you mean: what do I do with it?

MARY

I'm not used to presents like this.

CRICK

So?

MARY

What do I do with it?

CRICK

Look at it.

She looks at it.

MARY

Again and again?

CRICK

It's not like: again and again.

Crick puts a chair in front of the painting. Mary sits and looks at it.

MARY

I know, but—

CRICK

It's good practice to just *look* at something. If Eve had just looked at that apple instead of eating it, we'd all be better off. If all the bad things of the world were paintings, and we just looked at 'em, we'd be better off. It clears your head, just to look at something. Don't you think?

MARY

But how many times, I wonder?

CRICK

What?

MARY

I mean, if you own your own painting, how many times a day should you look at it?

CRICK

As many times as you want.

They look at the painting.

Doesn't it clear your head?

MARY

Yeah.

Mary stands in front of the painting, posing.

How long do you think you could just look at me, without kissing me?

CRICK

Not too long.

MARY

Try.

> *He looks at her for a while.*
> *He kisses her.*

CRICK

Merry Christmas, Mary.

MARY

Merry Christmas. I love the painting. I really do.

8. Crick Looks at His Painting

Crick puts the painting on the wall.
He looks at it.
He puts it on a different wall.
He looks at it.
He puts it on the floor.
He looks at it.
He does a push-up over it and looks at it.
He rolls over on his back.
He holds the painting above him.
He looks at it.
He puts it on the ground beside him.
He curls up next to it.
He looks at it.

9. Mary Makes Soup

Mary's kitchen, overlapping with previous scene.
She thumbs through the Joy of Cooking.
Her excitement mounts as the process becomes more and more violent.

MARY

"Consommé: a clear soup."
There it is!
"A clear soup is supposed to be as bracing as a clear conscience."
How about that. I've thought the very same thing. I wonder who
wrote this cookbook.

She looks to see who wrote the cookbook.

Never heard of her.
"About clear soups: because so much valuable material and expert
time go into the making of clear soups and because they taste so
delicious, most of us assume that they have high nutritional value."
Yes, I do.
"It disappoints us to have to tell you that, while they are unsur-
passed as appetite stimulators, the experts give them an indiffer-
ent rating as food."
That can't be right.
"Instead of calling for things young and tender, remember that
meat from aged animals and mature vegetables will be most fla-
vorsome. *Bones are disjointed and crushed*; meat is trimmed of fat
and cut up. Bones, especially marrow bones with *gelatinous extrac-
tives*, play an important role in stock.
As the stock heats, quite a heavy scum rises to the surface. If a clear
soup is wanted, push the scummy *albuminous* crust to one side.
Continue simmering. Again, push the scummy foam to one side.
Add lean ground beef, one egg white and crumpled shell, and *several uncooked fowl carcasses*. Beat these additions into the stock."
My God.
It's violent, isn't it?

Mary fills a pot with water and puts it on the stove.
Crick looks at Mary.

10. Mary and Red, Outside the City Limits

Red eats soup out of a thermos.

RED

I think you've done it, Mary. Just like in the restaurant.

MARY

Really?

RED

Yep. Dee-licious. How'd you do it?

MARY

You don't want to know.

RED

Why?

MARY

It was ugly.

RED

Guess things have to get ugly before they get nice.

MARY

Yeah.
Red. You're not afraid of what anyone thinks of you, are you?

RED

Nope. Not really.

MARY

How'd you get like that?

RED

I dunno.

MARY

Is it because your name is Red? I remember, in high school, you always wore these red velour pants. They were the ugliest things I'd ever seen.

RED

I loved those pants.
I wore 'em every day. I wore 'em until I wore the crotch clear out.
And then I bought another pair.

Red laughs.
Mary laughs.
They laugh about nothing in particular.
Then they stop.

MARY

Lately—I can't decide simple things, like should I eat this potato chip or should I take a walk. So I ask myself questions in my head. I close my eyes and ask: should I take a walk? And the voice answers: yes or no, and I think it's my own voice, but I'm not sure. Sometimes I think it's God's voice. But I've never been sure about God. So it must be my voice. Do you ever do that?

RED

Nope.

MARY

If you want to eat something, you eat it.

RED

I reckon so.

MARY

And if you want to take a walk, you take a walk.

RED

I do.

MARY

You don't think about it beforehand.

RED

Nope.

MARY

That's nice.

RED

I think about some things beforehand.

MARY

Like what?

RED

Never mind.
Maybe you think about things too much, Mary. You should learn to ride a horse. When you're riding a horse, there's no time to think, should I jump over this fence or shouldn't I? All of a sudden you're just jumping over a fence. You know?

MARY

But life isn't like that. Life is—

RED

What?

MARY

I don't know. I'm afraid of horses.

11. New Year's Eve

Crick watches It's a Wonderful Life *on television.*
Mary enters.

From an unseen television:

HARRY

"A toast . . . to my big brother, George. The richest man in town!"

The crowd breaks into cheering. People sing "Auld Lang Syne."

MARY

This is on again? This was just on.

CRICK

Shhh . . . I love this movie.

MARY

Don't you want to go to my mother's house? She's all alone.

CRICK

In a little bit. It's about to end.

Mary picks up the phone. She dials a number.
Crick turns up the volume.

MARY

Happy New Year! How's your leg? We're just watching a movie.
No—we didn't feel like going out. Crick? You want to talk?

CRICK

Just a second! It's my favorite part.

MARY

He says Happy New Year. Okay, Mom, I love you, too. Bye.

She dials another number.

Hello? Hi. Happy New Year!

Pause.

With the horses?

CRICK

Who's that?

MARY

It's Red. Want to wish her a happy New Year?

CRICK

No.

MARY

Okay, you too, bye.

From television:

ZUZU

"Look, Daddy. Teacher says, every time a bell rings an angel gets his wings."

GEORGE

"That's right, that's right."

Crick and Mary watch the movie. Crick is moved.

MARY

You crying, Crick?

CRICK

A little bit.

12. A Journal Entry

Morning light.
Mary takes her journal out from under the couch.
She unlocks her journal.
To the audience:

MARY

January 1. New Year's Resolutions. One: Write in Journal Every Day. Two: Read books about how to be a good mother and how to improve your sex life. Three: Learn to ride a horse.

Thoughts for the day: Bad things could happen. Your heart could stop ticking inside your body. Your husband could drop dead and you could find him laying there, his face blue. A window could fall on you. Some people have defective hearts that just stop ticking. There's nothing you can do. I might have one of those hearts. I might drop dead at any moment. Some people spontaneously burst into flames. No warning.

My life is not so bad. I read somewhere in a book: you have a right to be happy. Or was it: you have the right to pursue happiness. That's right. You have the right to *chase* happiness.

13. Red: A Song

RED

Oh, the sky doesn't worry me at night
Oh, the fly doesn't worry me in flight
My head doesn't worry me
My heart doesn't worry me
My forehead has no worry lines at all . . .

14. Crick and Mary Go to the Museum

CRICK

We'll start at the beginning. With the Middle Ages.

MARY

I thought we were starting at the beginning.

CRICK

It's the beginning of Western art.

MARY

I was just kidding—get it?

CRICK

That's pretty good!

MARY

Thanks.

CRICK

Used to be they painted people flat.
Like this.
Do you like it?

MARY

Everyone looks so—sad—
with blood coming out everywhere.
And flat.
Like someone ran over the Virgin Mary with the great big machine
they use to clean ice at a skating rink.

CRICK

Let's go to the next room. You'll like that better.
Modern art.

They look at a new set of paintings.

Which one's your favorite?

MARY

I don't know yet.

CRICK

Well, pick your favorite inside your head and then I'll guess it.

MARY

That's a good game. Okay.

CRICK

You picked?

MARY

Yes.

CRICK

Is it that one?

MARY

No.

CRICK

That one?

MARY

No.

CRICK

That one was my favorite.

MARY

Why didn't you guess it first? You didn't think we'd have the same
favorite?

CRICK

Aw, Mary. How about that one?

MARY

Nope.

CRICK

I'm stumped.

MARY

It's that one. The one of flowers.

CRICK

Really?

MARY

Yeah.

CRICK

That's not even a famous one.

MARY

It must be kind of famous. It got picked for a museum.

CRICK

I've never heard of the painter.

MARY

Do you like it?

CRICK

Your one?

MARY

Yeah. Do you think it's pretty?

He pauses to look at it.

CRICK

I don't like paintings of flowers. Usually. But I like this one.
Yes. I definitely do.
It reminds me of you.

MARY

So your favorite is that one.

CRICK

Yes.

MARY

Huh.

CRICK

What—you don't like it?

MARY

No—it's just that . . . if I were painting that woman, I would make
her arms longer. Her arms look—funny.

CRICK

Honey, it's on purpose. It's modern art. Things don't look the way they really look in life.

MARY

Oh.

CRICK

Now do you like it?

MARY

Is it supposed to be pretty? To make a woman look deformed like that?

CRICK

It's—making a statement.

MARY

My stomach hurts.

CRICK

Do you want me to rub it?

MARY

Not in the museum. People would stare.

CRICK

Do you want to see the Greek art? You might like that better. The women's arms will be the right size.

MARY

That might make me feel better.

CRICK

Or we could head over to contemporary art. You could see my favorite painting in the entire world.

MARY

What's it called?

CRICK

Untitled.

She doubles over in pain.

MARY

Oh!

CRICK

What is it?

MARY

I think I might be having the baby.
Oh!
Crick! Lay me on that bench. Oh!

CRICK

Hold it in, Mary! Hold it in! Oh, honey! Is there a doctor!

1 5 . Mary on the Phone at the Hospital

MARY

Hi, Mom. It's a girl! Yeah. Just like I thought. When she came out of me, Crick yelled: it's a boy! Because he saw the umbilical cord which was sort of big, but then the doctor said no, that's the umbilical cord, you have yourself a girl.
So—something weird happened at the hospital. No, nothing like that. I haven't told anyone, okay? So don't act weird about it.
When I was holding the baby—a doctor came in and said to me: There's something urgent.
We aren't sure if the baby's a boy or a girl.
Hold on. Just listen, Mom.
I said: what? How is that possible?
They said: it's sort of like a boy and a girl too.
There are some implications, they said. We're going to do a little surgery. No need to tell the baby. And then they did a little surgery.

Crick got—upset. But the doctors said: everything will be fine.
So I guess it's a girl now. I don't know why they couldn't have left
well enough alone.
It's beautiful, Mom. The baby.

Pause. The mother asks a question.

Oh, no, we don't have one yet.
I want to call her Blue.

16. Song

Red sings a song on her guitar.
Mary cradles the baby.

RED

Who will cradle the mouse to sleep?
The cat will.
Who will cradle the sun to sleep?
The moon will.
Who will cradle the moon to sleep?
The sky will.
Who will cradle the sky to sleep?
The cowboys will.
Oh, who will cradle the sky to sleep?
The cowboys will.
The cowboys will.

A horse walks across the stage.
Red gets on the horse and rides off.

A real horse would be nice.
An abstract approximation of the horse will do.
End of Part 1.
Intermission. Or not.

PART 2

||||⟡||||

I.

Mary nurses the baby.
She and the baby are bathed in light, like a Swedish painting.
Crick watches them.

CRICK

Look at you. Beautiful. The two of you.

MARY

Aw, Crick.

CRICK

I'm gonna take your picture.

> *He arranges the lamplight around Mary's head.*
> *He takes their picture.*
> *Crick holds the camera out in front of him*
> *and takes a picture of the three of them.*

Our little family.

They rest for a moment
in the idea of being a family.

MARY

Crick.

CRICK

Yeah?

MARY

We gotta decide her name soon.

CRICK

Yeah. I know.

MARY

She'll grow up weird, if she doesn't have a name.

CRICK

I know. That's what I keep telling you, honey. But I'm not calling
her Blue.

MARY

I'm not calling her Jill.

CRICK

So let's keep calling her Baby.

MARY

The more I look at her the more she looks like her name is Blue.
Like those blue flowers at our wedding—remember?

CRICK

Look, I'm not calling my child Blue Thorndigger! That's weird.
I told you. Kids at school would make fun of her.

MARY

Well then I'll keep calling her Blue and you keep calling her Jill.
That's all there is to it.

CRICK

She's going to get confused.

MARY

I'm with her more than you are. She'll get used to Blue.

CRICK

You're so fucking underhanded. Whispering names in the baby's
ear. Like a spy for the Chinese government. You and your Chinese
soup. *(Pause)* Just kidding.

MARY

Not in front of the baby.

CRICK

Sorry.

MARY

She won't feel like herself if we call her Jill—she'll feel—off—
she'll search and search for her real intended name—and then
one day—I'll tell her—your real name is Blue—but by then she'll
be disfunctioned. Because everyone is named Jill. And she's not
like everyone.

CRICK

No, she's not like everyone.
Things are going to be weird enough, without her having a weird
name.

MARY

Things aren't going to be weird. Things are going to be—fine.

CRICK

Yeah.

Mary puts the baby in a bassinet.
Crick begins building a temporary sculpture out of household objects.

MARY

Crick. I want that five hundred dollars back.

CRICK

What? Why? We're married. We share everything now.

MARY

I want to buy a stroller for Blue.

CRICK

I bet you could get a used stroller for fifteen dollars at the Salvation Army. I'll give you fifteen dollars.

MARY

But I want that particular money. The five hundred dollars you borrowed from me.

CRICK

Why?

MARY

The baby's going to need a lot of things. I want my savings. Just in case.

CRICK

Mary. Our money is the same money now. The day we got married, our bodies became one body and our money became one big money. You can't tell it apart. Each separate bill of green is—conjoined—one to the other—like—blades of grass—made into one holy field.

MARY

That's beautiful, Crick.

CRICK

Besides, I invested it.

MARY

What?

CRICK

Yeah, I invested it.

MARY

How do you know how to invest anything?

CRICK

You calling me dumb?

MARY

No.

CRICK

I invested it. In the painting I bought for you.

MARY

That was five hundred dollars?

CRICK

It's an investment. One day that painter will be discovered, and
we'll be rich.

MARY

Oh, no.

CRICK

You have to believe in invisible things, Mary, like investments.
Your problem is you don't believe in money unless it's right in
front of you. Imagine—the value of a painting can grow—invisi-
bly. It's like a marriage, just sitting there, every year, growing in
value, the longer you keep it. Until one day, you have a golden
anniversary.

MARY

You idiot. Paintings don't make a person rich.

CRICK

Did you just call me an idiot?

MARY

I'm sorry. I didn't mean it.

He makes his hand into a fist at his side.

Don't hit me.

CRICK

I wasn't going to hit you. Are you crazy?

MARY

I don't know. Am I?

CRICK

Mary.

MARY

If you hit me I'll ride a horse out of town. I will.

CRICK

Mary. What is *wrong* with you?
I bought that painting for you.

2. The Stables, Outside the City Limits

Red is teaching Mary to ride a horse.
It would be nice if it were a real horse.
If not, an abstract approximation of a horse will do.

RED

Wanna get up?

MARY

He's so—big.

RED

You gotta remember that horses are big old 'fraidy cats. They're flight animals.

MARY

I think I'm a flight animal.

RED

Nah—he doesn't see you that way.

MARY

You sure?

RED

Yeah.
Now, gimme your foot . . .
One, two, three . . . swing your right leg over!

Red gives Mary a leg up.

MARY

Whoah!

RED

Hold the reins!
You don't wanna get onto a horse and not hold the reins.
That would be—unadvisable.

Mary takes hold of the reins.

Are you ready for a ride?

MARY

Yes I am!

RED

Good.

MARY

Oh—but I have to pick up the baby from my mother's in an hour.
Before Crick gets home from work.

RED

Don't worry. That's plenty of time. We can climb over that crick
on the other side of the hill.

MARY

We're going to cross the water?

RED

You're gonna love it!

MARY

Won't the horse slip on the rocks?

RED

Nah. Don't be a 'fraidy cat, Mary.
He's the 'fraidy cat. *(Gesturing to the horse)*
You gotta be brave. You're the cowboy.

MARY

I'm the cowboy.

RED

That's right. Show no fear.

MARY

No fear! All right! I'm gonna kick him! Sorry, horse! Here I go!

RED

You got it, Mary!

MARY

Are you following me?

RED

I'm right behind you.

In slow motion,
Mary swings her arm overhead
as she and her horse ride offstage.

MARY

Yeeeee-haaaa!

Kick-ass cowboy music.

3. Veteran's Day

Mary comes home from riding a horse.
She gets out her journal.
She writes in her journal,
something secret and beautiful.
She makes up a metaphor.
She looks around to see if anyone's
overheard her metaphor.
Crick walks in.
She leaves her journal on the table.
She puts a magazine on top of it.

MARY

What are you doing home from work so early?

CRICK

It's Veteran's Day. I went to work and they sent me home.

MARY

Oh. Welcome home!

CRICK

Let's make love, honey, it's Veteran's Day!

They embrace.

MARY

What's gotten into you?

CRICK

This morning I was out of deodorant so I put your deodorant on
and I smelled like you all day and it turned me on to smell myself.

He kisses her.

Hey—are you wearing eye makeup?

Mary is wearing eye makeup.

MARY

No.

CRICK

You are. Did you go out today?

MARY

No.

CRICK

Why'd you put on eye makeup, to be home all day?

MARY

I told you, I'm not wearing eye makeup.

CRICK

Come here. Let me see. Is that eye shadow?

MARY

No!

CRICK

Aw, Mary.
Come here, you.
How often do I have a day off?

He kisses her.
He inspects her eyes for eye makeup.
He licks his finger and tries to remove the eye shadow.
He embraces her on the couch.

4. A Song

RED

The story is old
'Bout a man and a woman
With hearts as red as mine.

Oh, he gave her a cactus
And she broke his he-art
And left him in the road
To—o cry—y—y.

Are you blue tonight, honey?
Are you all by your lonesome,
Is your cactus dry tonight?

Are you blue tonight, honey?
Are you blue by your lonesome,
Did your cactus dry up and die?

5. Veteran's Day: One Hour Later

Mary and Crick sit on the sofa.
Their clothes are mussed.

MARY

What is Veteran's Day, anyway?

CRICK

It's for veterans.

MARY

There are—so many holidays these days.

CRICK

We've always had Veteran's Day.

MARY

Well it *seems* like a lot—they come—one after the other, like a flock of terrible birds.

CRICK

Huh?

MARY

(On the verge of tears) And you're supposed to be celebrating, but you don't understand what you're celebrating, and you don't know who made up Veteran's Day, you don't even understand the *word*.

CRICK

You don't know what a veteran is?

MARY

Sure I know what a veteran is. But Labor Day—I mean what the hell is that?

CRICK

It's for workers.

MARY

But—*why?*

CRICK

So they don't have to work.

MARY

Labor Day sounds like they *are* working. It's stupid.

CRICK

I don't know what's gotten into you, Mary. It's not healthy, you staying home with the baby all day.

MARY

Well, I'm not going back to work!

CRICK

I wasn't suggesting that.

MARY

Then what were you suggesting?

Pause.

CRICK

I lost my job.

MARY

What?

CRICK

I got fired.

MARY

Why?

CRICK

I touched—a painting.

MARY

What?

CRICK

At the museum is this painting of just the color red and white. Red on top and white on the bottom. You look at it and you just want to cry your eyes out—you don't know why. I look at it all day. I watch the people go by. They look at the painting and they are unmoved. It's like they have plastic flowers for souls. Sometimes I stay late just to look at it. Today was its last day. Then it goes far away.

I had to touch it. The paint is so thick. An inch thick. Or more. I wasn't going to hurt it. I waited for a holiday. I turned off the alarm. And I touched it. There was another alarm I didn't know about. It kept ringing. People came running. And you know what? It was worth it. To touch the paint.

Pause.

MARY

How could you be so dumb?

CRICK

Don't call me that! Why'd you call me that?

Crick curls up in a ball and cries.
Mary comforts him.

MARY

I'm sorry. I didn't mean it.

She cradles him.

CRICK

What are we going to do, Mary?

MARY

We'll get by.
When do you stop working?

CRICK

Today.

MARY

When do they stop paying you?

CRICK

Today.
We'll have more time at home together.
You, me, the baby. That'll be nice. Won't it?

MARY

Yeah. That'll be nice.

6. A Pasture Outside the Stables

Mary and Red watch untamed colts in a field.

RED

You cold?

MARY

No, I'm fine.

Red gives Mary her denim jacket.

Thanks.

Red tips her hat.

So those are the little ones? What do you call 'em?

RED

Colts.

MARY

Colts. That's right. Look at that one.

RED

She's a nasty one. She'll take a while to break.
Usually girls are quicker.

MARY

You ever broken a wild horse?

RED

Yeah.

MARY

How'd you do it?

RED

There are lots of ways.

MARY

But how do *you* do it?

RED

You really want to know?

MARY

Yeah.

RED

Okay. Well, horses are afraid to be alone. If they do something bad, you make them stay away from the group. When they start behaving again, you invite them back. You make 'em leave and come back, leave and come back, leave and—

MARY

Come back.

RED

Yeah. Every time they come back, they're more tame.

MARY

How do you make a horse leave?

RED

You stare at 'em funny—make 'em afraid.

MARY

Like this?

Mary stares at Red. Red laughs.

RED

Kinda.

MARY

Why does a horse come back?

RED

For some reason, they want to be close to the person who's chasing them.

MARY

Why?

RED

Once a horse loves you, he'll do anything for you.

MARY

How d'you make a horse love you?

RED

They just do.

MARY

You ever been in love—with a person?

RED

Naw. I'm not much for people.

MARY

Why?

RED

Always seemed—kinda mean—always talking—always trying to get up a hill or push someone down a hill. Horses are so damn smart. Nice too. You know any people who are nice and smart both?

Mary thinks.

See?
And horses—so quiet—in the night—their tails going—nothing more peaceful in the world. I tell you.

MARY

Yeah.

RED

You and Crick fell in love real early, huh? When your hearts were
busting out of your overalls? What was it—in the second grade?

MARY

Yeah—it was second grade.

RED

How do you know if you love someone in the second grade?

MARY

Oh, we knew.
We have the same birthday.
It was—fate.

RED

Hey, Mary?

MARY

Yeah?

RED

Do you mind if we just sit and don't talk for a while?
Sometimes I like just to sit and not to talk.

MARY

Sure. I'll try it, I guess.

They sit and don't talk. The sun sets. They watch it.

That's pretty.
Oh—sorry. We're not talking, are we?

RED

That's okay. You say whatever pops into your head.

The sun sets some more.

MARY

There's no shadow over any part of it.

RED

Huh?

MARY

With you—not talking.

RED

Aw, Mary.

MARY

Let's do it some more. The not talking. I like it.

Red nods.
The sun completely sets.

7. The Horse Ride to the Front Door

Crick waits for Mary to come home.
He looks at his watch.
He looks at the magazines on the coffee table.
He sees Mary's journal.
He looks at the cover.
He puts it down.
He picks it up.
He reads it.
He is disturbed.
He hears the sound of horse's hooves coming from outside.
He looks out the window.
He sees Mary riding up to the front door on a horse.
Mary enters.

MARY

Hi.

CRICK

What the—

MARY

I got a ride.

CRICK

Yeah! I saw!

MARY

I got a ride home.

CRICK

Mary! Riding a horse to our *front* steps—as though that were a perfectly *natural* thing to do—JESUS GOD IN HEAVEN!

MARY

You'll wake the baby.

CRICK

So let's all wake up—you, me, the baby! Because, Mary, the unexamined life is not worth living. I've had it with your antics.

MARY

I haven't done anything wrong.

CRICK

You're late!

He throws a pot against the wall.

MARY

I know. I'm sorry.

CRICK

I've been waiting for you since the second grade.

MARY

You have me.

CRICK

A woman who *respects* her husband does not ride a *horse* up to his
front door with another *man*—

MARY

Woman—

CRICK

For all the neighbors to see!
Who was that?

MARY

Red.

CRICK

It looked like a man.

MARY

I told you. She's a cowboy.

CRICK

I read your journal.

MARY

You what?

CRICK

I read your journal.

MARY

How could you?

CRICK

I was home all day, waiting for you. I wondered what you were
thinking about. I thought maybe there was something nice in it—
about us.

MARY

Did you read the whole thing?

CRICK

No.

MARY

What parts?

CRICK

You were riding a horse.

MARY

When?

CRICK

On Veteran's Day. You said you were home all day. Why did you lie to me?

MARY

I don't know. I was afraid.

CRICK

Why would you be afraid of me? Have I ever hurt you?

MARY

No.

CRICK

So then why?

MARY

I don't know.

CRICK

All I ever asked of you was a little honesty!

He throws a loaf of bread against the wall.
She starts crying.

Stop crying!

MARY

Why?

CRICK

I can't be mad at you if you're crying!

MARY

I'm sorry.
I'm going to my mother's.

CRICK

Don't go.

MARY

YOU READ MY JOURNAL!

CRICK

I'm sorry. That was bad of me.

MARY

You can't ever do that again.

CRICK

I won't. I promise.
Mary—no one will ever love you as much as I love you.

Kissing her.

I love you I love you I love you I love you I love you I love you.

MARY

I love you, too.

CRICK

You still leaving?

MARY

Yeah. I need to take a walk.

CRICK

Whaddya mean, a walk?

MARY

To my mother's.

CRICK

That's a seven-hour walk.

MARY

Yeah.
Take care of Blue.

CRICK

What? When will you be back?

MARY

I don't know.
Good-bye.

She leaves, holding her journal.

CRICK

We were supposed to ride off into the sunset together, Mary.
We were.

8. Red Sings a Song on Her Guitar

RED

Leave, leave, leave while you're able
Don't you have an overgrown heart
Don't you have an overgrown stable.

Learn how to ride
'Fore you learn how to speak
Your legs will be strong
When your ear it is weak.

9. Thanksgiving

Crick watches It's a Wonderful Life, *holding the baby.*
From an unseen television:

GEORGE

"Now you listen to me! I don't want any plastics! I don't want any
ground floors, and I don't want to get married—ever—to anyone! You understand that? I want to do what *I* want to do. And
you're . . . you're . . . Oh, Mary . . . Mary . . ."

MARY

"George . . . George . . . George . . ."

GEORGE

"Mary."

The phone rings.

CRICK

Hello? Oh, hi Mrs. Smith. Mom. No—she's not home. I thought
she was with you. I don't know where she is. Probably outside the
city limits. At the stables. She's learning to sleep standing up. Oh,
just a joke. Well, Happy Thanksgiving to you, too, Mrs. Smith.
Okay, then. Uh—wait—you have any friends over for dinner?

Well, you could come over here if you want. I have ingredients for
turkey sandwiches. No—it wouldn't be a bother at all. Okay, then.
Bye now.

He turns off the television.
He starts preparing two turkey sandwiches, holding the baby.

All righty, Jill. We're going to make some sandwiches. Are you
Daddy's little girl? Aw, yes, yes you are. That's right, honey.

Mary walks in.

MARY

Crick?

CRICK

Mary.

MARY

Blue.

They embrace, as in the scene we just heard from It's a Wonderful
Life. *The baby witnesses their reunion, stuck inside their embrace.*

Oh, Crick.

CRICK

Oh, Mary, Mary, Mary . . .
I want to kiss every inch of you.
I want to look at every inch of you.

MARY

Oh, Crick.

Mary takes the baby from Crick.

Oh, Blue. I missed you, honey.
Is she all right?

CRICK

I want to kiss your hands!
And your feet.
And your stomach.
Put her down for a second.

Mary puts the baby down.
Crick devours Mary with kisses.

That was the longest we've been apart since the second grade.
It was torture.

MARY

Kiss me like in the movies.

They kiss.

CRICK

You back for good?

MARY

Yeah.

CRICK

Oh, Mary.

MARY

Oh, Crick.

They embrace some more.

CRICK

Did you miss me?

MARY

Of course I did.

CRICK

Where were you?

MARY

My mother's.

CRICK

She just called.
She was wondering where you were.

MARY

I was walking.

CRICK

Just walking?

MARY

I couldn't eat, I couldn't sleep. So I walked. Home.

CRICK

Aw, honey. Do you remember when I first knew I loved you?

MARY

Tell me again.

CRICK

It was our eighth birthday. We were supposed to blow out the candles on our cupcakes at the same time. But you were so beautiful, I couldn't blow out my candles. I just kept looking at you.

MARY

Oh, Crick.

CRICK

Let's have cupcakes tonight, to celebrate.

MARY

Okay.

Crick moves to get ingredients for cupcakes.
He stops.

CRICK

Mary?

MARY

Yeah.

CRICK

I don't want you seeing that cowboy anymore, okay?

MARY

Why?

CRICK

I want to live a harmonious life. No cowboys, no Indians, just you and me. What do you say?

MARY

She's my friend.

CRICK

But I'm your husband. That's more important than a friend. I need you to promise me.

A pause.

MARY

All right.

CRICK

So you're staying?

MARY

Yeah.

CRICK

Stick with me, honey. From now on, every day is going to be like a holiday!

PART 3: The Holidays

The following sequence of scenes builds in speed until it is faster than real time.

1. Birthday

Mary and Crick sing to the baby:

MARY

Happy birthday to you,
Happy birthday to you,
Happy birthday dear Blue
Happy birthday to you.

CRICK

Happy birthday to you,
Happy birthday to you,
Happy birthday dear Jill
Happy birthday to you.

2. St. Patrick's Day

CRICK

I brought home shamrock shakes from McDonalds's. For St. Patrick's Day.

MARY

Wow. They're green.

3. Birthday

MARY

Happy birthday, Crick.

CRICK

Happy birthday, Mary.

MARY

On the same day—

CRICK

Of the same month—

MARY

Of the same year—

CRICK

Your mother—

MARY

And your mother—

CRICK

Holding us—

MARY

At the same time.

CRICK AND MARY

Happy birthday.

4. Valentine's Day

CRICK

Happy Valentine's Day, honey.

MARY

Should we go to church?

CRICK

For Valentine's Day?

MARY

Isn't he a saint?

CRICK

Yeah.

MARY

We never go to church. Why don't we go to church?

CRICK

We're not religious.

MARY

Oh. Yeah.

5. Christmas

MARY

Christmas is early this year.

CRICK

Christmas is always the same day.

MARY

Isn't there a holiday that comes early? Depending on the month, or the Leap Year, or the moon?

CRICK

I don't know what you're thinking of.

Mary looks out the window.

MARY

It's snowing.

Crick sings:

CRICK

I'm dreaming of a White Christmas,
Just like the ones I used to know . . .
May your days be merry and bright!

MARY AND CRICK

And may all your Christmases be white . . .

MARY

I hope the firecrackers don't scare the baby.

6. Groundhog Day

CRICK

Happy Groundhog Day, Mary.

MARY

No shadow.

7. Halloween

Mary, looking out the window.

MARY

The trick-or-treaters never come to our house.
I wish more children lived on this street.

CRICK

We could have another.

8. Fourth of July

Crick lights Mary's sparkler with his sparkler.
They wave their sparklers.

9. Anniversary

CRICK

Happy anniversary, Mary.

MARY

Merry birthday, Crick.
Merry or happy?

CRICK

Happy.

MARY

Merry or happy?

CRICK

Happy.

MARY

Have a—
Have a—holiday.

CRICK

Happy—

MARY

What?

CRICK

Happy.

MARY

What?
Have a—

*From the television: the sound of the ball dropping in Time's Square
and the noisy crowd.
The volume is up high.
Crick shouts along with the television:*

CRICK AND CROWD

Ten, nine, eight, seven, six . . .

Shouting over the television:

MARY

New Year's is early this year.

CRICK

New Year's is always the same day.

Crick blows a noise-maker.

MARY

Can we turn it down?

Counting down:

CRICK AND CROWD

FIVE, FOUR, THREE, TWO, ONE! HAPPY NEW YEAR!

A collision of holiday sounds: horns, wedding bands, ho ho ho's, the sound of an Easter bunny, the sound of a groundhog, the sound of prayers.

10. Day After New Year's

Mary alone.
She throws out streamers, party hats
and three boxes of Kentucky Fried Chicken.

MARY

(To herself) I'm sick of holidays.
(To God) I'm sick of holidays!
(To the world) I'M SICK OF
FUCKING HOLIDAYS!!!!!!!

She sits down, surprised at herself. She breathes.

PART 4

||||⬚||||

1. Mary Calls Her Mother for Guidance

MARY

Mom? Hi, it's me. No, I'm fine. Mom, I was wondering. Did it ever happen to you, when you reached a certain age, that every day felt like a holiday? *(Pause)* No, not in a good way. I mean—I have no—recollection of the normal days—in between the holidays. Do you think having children could do this to you? Oh, the baby's fine. No, she doesn't know she's part boy yet. It's not like that. *(Pause. The mother says: well, what is it like?)* I don't know what it's like. She's just a baby. Thanks, Mom. Bye.

Mary sings a lullaby to the baby.
Red plays the guitar, in the background, accompanying Mary.

Who will cradle the sky to sleep?
The cowboys will.
Oh, who will cradle the sky to sleep?
The cowboys will.
The cowboys will . . .

Red takes up the song.

RED AND MARY

Oh, who will cradle the sky to sleep?

RED

The cowboys will.
The cowboys will . . .

2. A Journal Entry

Mary composes a journal entry. To the audience:

MARY

Dear Blue,

I'm writing you a letter, just in case, on the occasion of your birthday. Because sometimes I have a premonition that my heart is going to stop ticking. I don't know why—it's a premonition.

I wanted you to know, Blue, if you grow up to be a woman, and one day you start feeling kind of funny—like maybe you're a woman, but maybe you're not, I want you to know that you're not crazy. You're smart. And it's hard to grow up. Nature is—mysterious.

If I die, and you're in charge of my funeral, I want there to be cowboys. And cowboy songs. I want to be buried outside the city limits. And I want there to be Chinese soup. Clear broth. So everyone leaves with a clear head.

Does any of this make sense, Blue? I don't know why I'm writing this. I'll laugh about it when I'm seventy-two.

Love,
Your mother,
Mary

She locks the journal.

3 . Christmas

Crick puts up Christmas decorations.
A crèche, stockings, lights.
It's a Wonderful Life *is playing in the background:*

". . . I owe everything to George Bailey. Help him, dear father.
Joseph, Jesus and Mary, help my friend Mr. Bailey.
Help my son George, tonight.
He never thinks about himself, God. That's why he's in trouble.
George is a good guy. Give him a break, God.
I love him, dear Lord. Watch over him tonight.
Please, God, something's the matter with Daddy."

> *Mary enters from the bedroom.*
> *She watches Crick for a moment.*

CRICK

I'll rewind the movie for you.

MARY

Okay.

CRICK

You wanna help me with the stockings?

MARY

Sure.

CRICK

We'll have some eggnog, open stockings . . . how 'bout that?

MARY

Sounds nice.

CRICK

What's wrong?

MARY

Oh—it's nothing.

CRICK

I wrapped all the presents.

MARY

Thanks, honey. I'm sorry I—wasn't in the mood.

CRICK

I hid all of Jill's Santa presents. I wrapped the doll with special paper.

MARY

Aw, that's nice.
Crick.

CRICK

Yeah.

MARY

I've been thinking. Maybe we shouldn't give Blue so many girl presents.

CRICK

What do you mean?

MARY

The dolls, and the dresses.

CRICK

Why not?

MARY

Maybe we can get her some in-between presents.

CRICK

What do you mean?

MARY

Like some paints, or, I don't know, building blocks.

CRICK

Why?

MARY

Maybe we shouldn't— *make* her—like girl things, you know? If she doesn't want to.

CRICK

But she is a girl.

MARY

Kind of.

CRICK

I'm not having this discussion on Christmas Eve.

MARY

Then when?

CRICK

Later.

MARY

She's not a baby anymore.

CRICK

I know. She's a little girl.

MARY

But why does she have to be one thing or another?

CRICK

Because sometimes in life, Mary, you have to choose. You can't live on a fence. I won't have my daughter living on a fence.

Pause.

MARY

I don't feel like celebrating Christmas this year.

CRICK

What?

MARY

I don't want to celebrate Christmas.

CRICK

Not celebrate Christmas?

MARY

That's right.

CRICK

How can you not celebrate Christmas?

MARY

You just—don't—do it.

CRICK

Mary.

MARY

I'm going to go for a walk.

CRICK

You're going out for a walk—on Christmas Eve.

MARY

I know it's not—the thing to do. I'm sorry.

CRICK

What is it that you *want*?

MARY

I just want—to be with time, as it moves along.

CRICK

Aren't you doing that?

MARY

No. Time is going too fast. I want it to stop.

CRICK

Aw, honey. I know how you feel.

MARY

You do?

CRICK

Yeah. When I want time to slow down, I look at a painting.
Come here. Let's look at the painting together.

They look at the painting.
He holds her.
She tries.

Doesn't it clear your head?

MARY

It's not working.
I'm sorry.
I'm going to take a walk.

CRICK

When will you be back?

MARY

When will I be back?

CRICK

What TIME will you be back?

MARY

I have no idea.

CRICK

Mary, if you leave on Christmas Eve, things will never be the same.

MARY

I'll be back. Don't worry.

They look at each other.
She leaves.
He throws a wrapped present against the wall.

4. At the Green Shutters, Christmas Eve

Red pours Mary another glass of wine.
They are both a little drunk.

MARY

I wish I had a present for you.

RED

That's okay.

MARY

I'm not celebrating this year. I didn't wrap any presents.
Crick wrapped all the presents.

RED

I never wrap presents.

MARY

Never? How do you surprise people?

RED

I'm full of surprises.

MARY

I bet you are.

RED

I am.
Well. We forgot about our cookies.

They break open their fortune cookies.

MARY

What's yours?

RED

What's yours?

MARY

No, you first.

RED

Ladies first.

MARY

You're a lady.

RED

I'm no lady.

MARY

I guess you're not a lady like that.

RED

Nope.

MARY

You ever wonder about "ladies first"?
I wonder about "ladies first."

RED

What do you wonder?

MARY

I mean: when a man says, ladies first, and opens the door, and follows right behind you, I wonder if it's so he can look at your butt.

RED

Sounds about right.

MARY

I'd like to be a real lady. I'd like to always say the right thing—
like—if someone dies—a real lady says the right thing. She wears
the right clothes to the wake—she doesn't stand out but she looks
nice—with appropriate shoes—and she writes the right thing on
stationery to the bereaved person. She writes something that
makes them feel like carrying on with their life. No words crossed
out or misspelled. She has a clear mind and a clear heart. Clear—
like soup.

RED

I think *you* are a real lady.

MARY

No, I'm not.

RED

You are.

MARY

No, I don't wear the right things. I don't write the best thank-you
letters and death notes. I know I don't.

RED

Well, I think you're a true lady.

MARY

Well, thank you.

RED

See? A true lady knows how to accept a compliment.

MARY

I just did that, didn't I?

RED

Yeah.
(*Gesturing to the fortune cookies*) So. Like I said: ladies first.

MARY

Okay.

Mary opens it.
She is forlorn.

It's blank.

RED

Blank! That's terrible.
Let's get you another one.

MARY

No, no, don't bother.

RED

(To an unseen waitress) Excuse me, ma'am, my friend here—she got
a blank fortune cookie. Would it trouble you greatly—to give us
another one, please?
Thank you.
See? That wasn't so bad.

MARY

I'm embarrassed.

RED

Don't be embarrassed. It's your fortune—you paid for it.
Now. Open it.

Mary opens her second fortune cookie. It's blank again.

MARY

Oh . . .

RED

What is it? What's it say?

MARY

It's blank again.

She is on the verge of tears.

Oh, Red, am I going to die?

RED

Now, honey.
Don't cry.
These must be defective.

MARY

Well what does yours say?

RED

Mine? Don't worry about mine.

MARY

But they're not all defective. Yours has a fortune.

RED

Let's see here. Mine says:
a family is a thousand blessings.

MARY

Oh! I'm going to die, aren't I?

RED

Now, listen. I don't have a family. Our fortunes got mixed up.
You were s'posed to get mine, and I was s'posed to get yours.

Mary calms down.

MARY

Do you think so?

RED

I know so.

MARY

But I don't want you to have a blank one.

RED

To me—a blank fortune is . . . an open sky on the horizon. Fill in the blank. A fortune no one's ever written up ahead of time, because no one could imagine a life as strange and as beautiful as the horse you're about to jump on.

MARY

That's beautiful.

RED

Should we blow this pop stand?

MARY

Yeah.

RED

Now you're really late.

MARY

I don't care.

5. Outside the City Limits

The same night, toward morning.
Red, Mary and a horse in silhouette.

MARY

I've never seen anything like it. Those factories look like big magical tin soup cans. With light coming out the sides. I never knew factories could look so beautiful.

Red. Do you think it's possible for two people to experience time at the exact same speed?

RED

Yes I do.

MARY

How do you know?

RED

Try me.

MARY

What do you mean?

RED

(In low tones) Mary.

Here. I'll show you. Dance with me.

MARY

I can't dance.

They dance.

RED

Just a two-step.
There, that's it.

They dance.

MARY

I'm late.

RED

There's no such thing as late. *Slow down.*

They dance.

MARY

Are we in horse time now?

RED

Yeah.

MARY

No one's late in horse time, are they?

RED

No.

They dance, cheek to cheek.

6. You're Late

The same morning.
Crick is at the door, holding a baseball bat, very still.
Mary walks in the door.

CRICK

You're late.

She notices that Crick is holding a baseball bat.

MARY

What are you doing?

CRICK

Nothing.
Where were you? *Riding a horse?*

MARY

Yeah.

CRICK

All I ever asked from you was a little honesty!

They breathe.

MARY

Are you going to kill me?

He doesn't answer.

ARE YOU GOING TO KILL ME?

CRICK

I just want to talk.

MARY

Okay. Let's talk.

CRICK

Jill and I had a nice Christmas Eve.
Did you have a nice Christmas Eve?

MARY

Yeah.

CRICK

Mary. I don't think you have a soul. You don't have any feelings.
You just DO things. You're more like an animal. An ape, or a dog,
or a horse.

MARY

I didn't do anything wrong.

CRICK

You lied to me.
Let's make love.

MARY

Now?

CRICK

Yeah.

MARY

I don't want to.

CRICK

Why?

MARY

I just don't.

CRICK

Let's go in the bedroom. C'mon.

MARY

No. Put down the baseball bat.

Crick puts down the baseball bat.
He tries to kiss her. She winces.
He puts his hands on the back of her neck, hard.

What are you doing?

CRICK

Nothing.

MARY

Why are you putting your hands on my neck?

CRICK

I don't know.

He keeps his hands on the back of her neck.

MARY

TAKE YOUR HANDS OFF OF ME.

He takes his hands off her.

CRICK

You really don't love me, do you?

MARY

THAT'S BESIDE THE POINT.

Blue enters.
The audience doesn't see her.
Crick and Mary follow Blue with their eyes.
A silence.

CRICK

Well, look, honey, you're up just in time for Christmas breakfast.
We're going to fry some eggs and put on some bacon and then
open stockings.
What do you say?

Blue says nothing.

MARY

Take my hand, Blue.
We're going on a walk.

Mary holds out her hand to Blue.
The imaginary Blue goes to her mother.
Mary turns to Crick.

Good-bye.

She exits.

7. Coda

Mary and Red in a vast landscape,
like the end of a cowboy movie.
Red wears a cowboy hat.
Red reaches into the stroller and pulls out another cowboy hat.
She puts it on Mary's head.

Crick looks at his painting.
He carries the empty frame
to the edge of a vast landscape.
He holds it in the air,
framing a field of color.
He tilts the frame, crooked.

RED AND MARY

Singing:

Oh, as the sun sets
The horses do sleep
The fields they are long
And the crick it is deep . . .

Oh, find me a child
Who grows into a girl
Who rides like a man—
With a mask.

THE END

Melancholy
Play

a contemporary farce

What Melancholy is,
with all the kinds, causes, symptomes,
prognostickes, and severall cures of it.
In three Partitions, with their severall sections,
members and subsections.

—*The Anatomy of Melancholy*, 1632
Robert Burton (Democritus Junior)

This play is dedicated to everyone who,
at one point or another,
has traveled to an almond state.
And for Kirsten Deluca,
fellow traveler.

PRODUCTION HISTORY

Melancholy Play was first produced by the Piven Theatre (Joyce Piven, Artistic Director) in Evanston, IL, on June 28, 2002. The production was directed by Jessica Thebus; the set design was by John Dalton, the lighting design was by Lynne Koscielniak, the costume design was by Mary Trumbour, the sound design was by Micky York and original music was composed by Gregory Hirte with additional songs by Jeffrey Weeter; the stage manager was Elizabeth Grantner. The cast was as follows:

FRANK	Geoff Rice
TILLY	Polly Noonan
FRANCES	Amy Warren
JOAN	Gita Tanner
LORENZO	Scot Morton
MUSICIAN	Gregory Hirte

Melancholy Play was later produced in October 2002, at Princeton University in a production directed by Davis McCallum, with music by Michael Friedman.

Melancholy Play was also produced in June 2005, by The Echo Theater Company in Los Angeles in a production directed by Chris Fields, with music by Michael Roth.

How to Use the Set

Set pieces and found objects may remain on stage the entire time, as in a chamber piece, or a site-specific piece. Many scenes can be played on the same chaise, without creating confusion about where we are. The hair salon may be established with a stool; the tailor shop with a mannequin or the act of sewing. The cello player should not be hidden, although the actors seem never to notice him until the bitter end.

The actors use windows to gaze out of. These windows may be moveable or not; they may even be created with light. But they should be old-fashioned and beautiful. And they should frame, rather than obstruct, the actors.

The world of the play is less about scenic illusion and more about seamless entrances and exits, so that one scene floats into another, broken only by a quick *arrêt* (as in commedia) or tableau. In other words, the actors enact the transformations, rather than the furniture.

The Music

The music exists in a parallel world, scoring melancholy inside the head—an organ at a silent movie. The actors respond to the music as actors, rhythmically and tonally, but the characters never appear to notice the cello player.

It would be nice if the actor who plays Julian were from a country other than the United States. And he or she should be a very good cello player. And handsome, and brooding. If possible, Julian is a man. If not, women cello players are extremely acceptable.

Julian is on stage during the whole play. He is, perhaps, revealed at some points more than others. But there is no need to hide Julian.

The score is another character in this play, scoring transitions, underscoring dialogue, moving the actors into song, and creating an entire world. The score should be treated with the utmost musical, theatrical, and mathematical sensitivity. The music should be integrated early and often in rehearsal, rather than being the icing on the cake.

Scores from previous productions (Michael Friedman's, Gregory Hirte's, Michael Roth's, and Jeffrey Weeter's) are all brilliant. Rights available upon request (for information, contact Michael Friedman, c/o ICM, Thomas Pearson, 40 West 57th Street, 16th Floor, New York, NY 10019; ghirte@earthlink.net; roth-musik@aol.com; Jeffrey Weeter, c/o Bret Adams Ltd., Bruce Ostler, 448 West 44th Street, New York, NY 10036).

Costumes

I imagine that Joan wears an old-fashioned nurse's uniform. Even though we are in Illinois, there is a sense of the iconic and cinematic.

On Casting

Frances and Frank, we learn later in the play, are twins. However, in the world of this play, there is no need for twins to resemble each other. If your Frances and Frank look nothing alike, simply change this line on page 315: "TILLY: My God! You look exactly like her!" to "TILLY: My God! You look nothing like her!" or even: "TILLY: My God! You look a little bit like her!"

Notes on Tone

Melancholy in this play is Bold, Outward, Sassy, Sexy and Unashamed. It is not introverted. It uses, instead, the language of Jacobean direct address.

However, be sensitive to the moments of delicacy, fragility, and sadness inside of the farce.

Having said that, actors are encouraged to look out of the window often, climb in and out of windows, throw open balconies, throw themselves on couches.

When Tilly is sad, she is sad. When she is happy, she is happy. There is no judgment in the play about happiness being inferior to sadness or sadness being inferior to happiness. Tilly must reside openly and sincerely inside the emotional state, moment to moment.

The pace is often faster than real time. Transitions should hurtle.

A quick simple head turn to the audience and back again will help establish the tone, when called for. The audience knows the difference between being talked to and talked at. Talk to them, please.

The untranslatable words alluded to in the play (there is a word in Portuguese, there is a word in Japanese) all exist . . . find them, and read a great deal of sad lyric poetry out loud while rehearsing.

Don't be afraid of sincere melodrama.

The *amygdala* is the most important organ of emotion in the brain. It is shaped like an almond (hence its name, derived from the Greek for almond). One sits on each side of the brain, adjacent to the organ of autobiographical memory, the hippocampus. The hippocampus is shaped like a seahorse (hence its name, derived from the Greek for seahorse). The amygdala receives sensory input from all organs, including smell, and attaches emotional meaning to sensations. People lacking amygdalae cannot make emotional inferences about their experiences in the world. Seizures, uncontrolled electrical storms within the brain, can involve the amygdala and cause unusual emotional and sensory experiences—for example, a feeling of sadness or fear. Or: the smell of bitter almonds . . .

—A. Jaruwat, M.D.

Amongst its many inconveniences, some comforts are annexed to Melancholy: First, it is not catching . . .

—*The Anatomy of Melancholy*, 1632
Robert Burton (Democritus Junior)

Mandorla, Italian for almond, was an ancient symbol comprised of two overlapping circles, which become an almond shape when a line is drawn around the two circles, like so:

PART 1

1. Frank Offers Up His Defense

A spotlight on Frank. Frank, to the audience:

FRANK

I would like to propose to you—this evening—a defense of melancholy.

Cello music from Julian.

Proposition 1:
That melancholy is a necessary bodily humor—
that there is a certain amount of necessary mourning—
due to things that grow and pass—
rice, the moon, wheat, childhood, men's hats, tides on a marsh,
fingernails—
Which leads me to:

Proposition 2:
That melancholy
is a disappearing emotion—

there is no place for it in the afternoon—
out the window—to observe the passage of time—
we are depressed—
but are we melancholy?
Are we capable of melancholy?
Which leads me to:

Proposition 3:
If disavowed—
the repressed melancholia may lead to other disturbances of the
mind—
may I here remind you of the godmother who was not invited to
Sleeping Beauty's baptism—
she took revenge.
She took revenge!

Proposition 4:
That we must anatomize melancholy—
take stock of the causes:
stars a cause
love a cause
death a cause
morning a cause
afternoon a cause
evening a cause
the odd times in between morning afternoon and evening:
a cause.

No more cello music.
Frank looks out the window.

2. Tilly Asks Frank Why
He Is Like an Almond

Tilly walks up to Frank.
Frank's back is to Tilly.

Tilly taps Frank on the back.
Frank turns around.

TILLY

Why are you like an almond?

They look at the audience.
They exit.

3. The Unfeeling Lorenzo

Lorenzo has an unidentifiable Italian accent.

LORENZO

My name is Lorenzo.
You would think,
with a name like Lorenzo,
that I would feel great passions.
Sadness, violent anger,
unbridled lust.
But my lust is bridled or not at all.
My anger too is bridled.
And my sadness—there is a cap on it, so it cannot get out.
Lorenzo, who plays the harp, in the dark, you might think.
Lorenzo, with kisses like Mediterranean apples, you might think.
But no.
It is I: Lorenzo, the unfeeling.
The Unfeeling Lorenzo.
I am an orphan. I was found on the doorstep of a candy store.
I was raised on sweets, in an unspecified European country.
I felt myself to be European.
I spoke an unspecified European language.
I lived on a street with cobblestones.
I wore a tan scarf.
But I did not suffer like a European.
No. I was—happy.

One day my long-lost
mother appeared on the steps of the sweetshop.
She was wearing a black skirt and black gloves
and a little black veil.
I smiled at her.
My God, he smiles like an American! she said.
Like he's smiling for a picture!
How white his teeth are!
And how straight!
(It was very disconcerting,
as you might imagine,
, for my mother.)
How could I have given birth, she said,
to this child?
Suffering, she announced,
is a brand of citizenship!
Then she walked out the door.
So I moved to Illinois.
I feel—normal here.
People say: You have such understanding eyes,
Lorenzo.
I look into your eyes and I feel I can deposit my pain
right there—like a coin, into a hole.
I have an office.
It is here.
Come in.

Tilly enters Lorenzo's office.

So.

TILLY

So.

LORENZO

You went off the medication.

TILLY

Yes. I'm sorry about that.

LORENZO

Uh-huh. You're sorry. Good. So.
How are we feeling today?

TILLY

I don't know how you are feeling. I am feeling—melancholy.

LORENZO

And what does that feel like?

TILLY

I would like to die and be reborn as a mushroom.
I would like to stay warm and slightly damp.
I will release spores now and again when it suits my mood.

LORENZO

Tilly. I want for you to go on a new medication. It is a very good
medication. It will make you feel—very nice.

TILLY

Lorenzo. Can I call you Lorenzo?

LORENZO

Lorenzo is my name. Yes, it is!

TILLY

Lorenzo.
Cheerful people are the worst sort of people. They make noise
when they smile. Their teeth have little bells between the cracks.
When they smile, their teeth ring.

LORENZO

I am going to fold my arms now Tilly. *(He does)* It seems to me,
Tilly, that you don't want to get better. It seems to me that you
enjoy this "melancholy" of yours. In fact, you seem proud of it. A

little vain, even. It is my professional opinion that you feed your melancholy little sweetmeats, that you comb it, groom it, keep it as a pet dog. Why have you come to see me?

TILLY

The bank made me come. They don't like their employees to be melancholic.

LORENZO

But you—you like to be a melancholic employee?

TILLY

Not really. I'd rather work for myself. Open a shop. Perfume. Or hats.

LORENZO

Let me tell you a story, Tilly. A patient of mine—he thought if he urinated, he would flood his entire village. So he could not urinate! And this was very painful to him. So I tell him a little white lie, I say to him, "Sir, your whole village is on fire." And suddenly he feels free to urinate. He feels, through this ordinary physical activity, that he is saving his village again and again.

TILLY

Huh.

LORENZO

Are you afraid of putting out the fires?

TILLY

No.

LORENZO

Do you find me attractive, Tilly? Is that the problem?

TILLY

I don't think so.

LORENZO

We call it transference, Tilly.

TILLY

At the bank you can transfer money—from one account—to another. I don't do that.

LORENZO

It is normal to fall in love with me. It is "okay."

TILLY

I am not in love with you!

LORENZO

Okay. Okay!

TILLY

Lorenzo, why do you try to make people happy?

LORENZO

Because I, myself, am happy. Happiness is contagious. It's like a disease.

TILLY

Do you never long to be sad?

LORENZO

No.

TILLY

Do you never want to cry?

LORENZO

No!

A pause.
The sound of rain.

TILLY

It's raining out.

LORENZO

So it is.

TILLY

Let's put our hands in the rain.

They open the window and stick their hands out, feeling the rain.
Sad, stirring music, played by Julian on the cello.

Look at the rain—how it sticks to the flowers. There's a word in
Japanese for being sad in the springtime—a whole word just for
being sad—about how pretty the flowers are and how soon
they're going to die. I can't remember the word—

LORENZO

You are a very beautiful woman.

TILLY

Oh no.

LORENZO

Tilly—my mother abandoned me at a sweetshop.

TILLY

Why are you telling me this?

LORENZO

Because—the heavens have cracked open—I suddenly want to
tell you everything. I think I'm in love with you, Tilly. They say
that's what happens when you fall in love. You want to tell people
things. You especially want to tell them sad things. Hidden sad
things from the past. Something like: I was abandoned at a sweetshop in an unspecified European country. Tilly.

TILLY

I'm so sorry.

LORENZO

Don't be sorry. I want to tell you all the sad things, and then you
will know me better than other people know me and that means

we are reserved for one another. Because we made a reservation like at a restaurant like at a grand hotel and we made this reservation with a certain foreign currency made of secret sad information we told each other in private rooms—oh, I feel a weight on my chest. What have you done to me, Tilly? Why?

TILLY

I'm sorry, Lorenzo. This happens sometimes—to me. I should have warned you.

4. Frank and Frances's Account of Their Labor

Frank and Frances speak simultaneously when their text is written on corresponding lines. They gesture in parallel fashion. They address the audience:

FRANK	FRANCES
When I gave up accounting	When I gave up physics
	I found myself sitting in
	public places
I found myself sitting in	
public places	
	libraries, restaurants, movie
	theaters
I pretended	
	that I was accountable
to the other people in the room	
	and that furthermore
they were accountable	
	to me.
I lost my watch.	I lost my watch.
I didn't buy a new one.	I didn't buy a new one.
I enjoyed asking strangers:	
What time is it?	What time is it?

SARAH RUHL

FRANK *(continued)*

eleven o'clock.

FRANCES *(continued)*
And they always answered:
two o'clock.

They turn toward one another.

Thank you, I said.

Thank you, I said.

They turn away.

This could be repeated
over and over again.

This could be repeated
over and over again.

They turn toward one another.

What time is it?
Eleven o'clock.

What time is it?

Thank you.

You're welcome.

They turn away.

So reassuring.
To experience
the social contract
again and again.

So reassuring.
To experience
the social contract
again and again.

And so I became a tailor.

And so I opened a beauty salon.

Even when I was a child
I liked it
when strangers touched me
with clinical purpose—
people I was not related to.

Even when I was a child
I liked it
when strangers touched me
with clinical purpose—
people I was not related to.

Comforting—
the hem of my pants

Comforting—
my hair—wet—

242

FRANK *(continued)*	FRANCES *(continued)*
soft against my leg	soft against my shoulders
a stranger who cared	a stranger who cared
or seemed to care	or seemed to care
about my physical well-being.	about my physical well-being.
Not creepy, understand—	
	nothing untoward or
	perverse—
but gentle.	but gentle.
I could have been a prostitute	I could have been a prostitute
and gotten the same effect	and gotten the same effect
or a doctor maybe—	or a doctor maybe—
but no	but no
the touch should	the touch should
feel—off-hand	feel—off-hand—
	someone grazes your shoulder
	while they're doing something
	else . . .

The speed of their speech slows down slightly.

something peaceful	something peaceful
no big deal	no big deal
time slows down	time slows down
when you're hemming pants . . .	when you're cutting hair . . .

Pause.

Plus I like fabric	Plus I like hair
I've always liked fabric	I've always liked hair
how it looks	how it looks
how is smells	how it smells
how it hangs	how it hangs
how a good suit can improve	how a good haircut can improve
an ugly duckling's appearance	an ugly duckling's appearance
make them feel competent	make them feel competent
and unafraid.	and unafraid.

5. Tilly Goes to the Tailor

Tilly stands in front of the mirror.
She wears trousers underneath her gown.
Frank pins the hem of her pants leg.

TILLY

Why are you like an almond?

FRANK

Sorry?

TILLY

I wanted to ask you.

FRANK

You wanted to ask me—

TILLY

Why are you like an almond?

FRANK

Did you ask me this before?

TILLY

Yes. Three seconds ago.

FRANK

I mean another time? Further back? I'm having a sensation of déjà vu.

TILLY

I hate déjà vu. Do you want to sit down?

FRANK

No, that's okay. Can you tell me *why* I am like an almond?

TILLY

You are like an almond because
you are dry—like bark—
a hungry woman doesn't stuff her mouth with almonds
they don't fill a person up—
you eat one and your mouth goes dry—
like the moment before you want to kiss someone—

FRANK

Have we met somewhere—before I was hemming your trousers?

TILLY

I work at the bank.

FRANK

Oh!

TILLY

I give you your money. You ask for forty dollars. I give it to you in
two tens and one twenty.

FRANK

That sounds familiar.

TILLY

I put the money in your hands. You are always distracted. When
you leave, I watch you go. You always turn left.

FRANK

I do. I do turn left.

TILLY

I'm not mistaken then, it's you that we're discussing.

FRANK

Yes, I think it's me that we're discussing—

TILLY

Why do you always deposit your check in person? You can deposit
the check into a machine. Outside. Do you know that?

FRANK

Yes—I'm aware of that.

TILLY

So then why—

FRANK

I don't know. It's just what I've always done.

TILLY

I never use the machine either.

FRANK

You don't?

TILLY

No. I don't.

> *They look at each other.*
> *Then Frank looks away.*

Are you afraid of me?

FRANK

No—I don't think so.

> *Tilly moves and Frank jabs himself with a pin.*

Ouch!
Sorry.

TILLY

Do you think I want to crack you open with a mallet and look
inside you?

FRANK

No.

TILLY

Because that's exactly what I'd like to do to you.

FRANK

Look—I'm a tailor—I—

TILLY

I mean not in a violent sense. Just in the sense that—I have a Persian friend. He once said to me: American men only have two emotions—happy and mad.

Frank stops tailoring.

FRANK

I'm not like that.

TILLY

I know.
You get sad—just by looking at the way light comes in through the window. In the afternoon maybe.

FRANK

I do.

TILLY

You do?

FRANK

I do. What's wrong?

TILLY

It's just that—
everyone is always coming and going.
I wish they would stay in one place.
At the bank—after they get their money—

customers—leave.
I stay—I stay there all day!
I think—that they think—
that I disappear until the next transaction—
well I don't! I stay!
In the mind of God—everything happens—
perpetually—God thinks about us all the time,
he keeps us alive, just by thinking about us—
well that's like me!
I THINK ABOUT MY CUSTOMERS ALL THE TIME.

She is on the verge of tears.

FRANK

I'm so sorry.

TILLY

No, you're not!

FRANK

I am, really! You seem—a little—sad—are you—sad?

TILLY

Sometimes.

FRANK

I don't mind. I like that, actually.

A pause. They look at each other.
Stirring sad music,
played by Julian, on the cello.

TILLY

There's a word in Portuguese—I can't remember the name—it
means melancholy—but not exactly—it means you are full of
longing for someone who is far away—

FRANK

I know that word.

TILLY

What is it.

FRANK

I can't remember.
Kiss me.

TILLY

You don't even know my name.

FRANK

What is your name?

TILLY

Tilly.

FRANK

Kiss me, Tilly.

TILLY

I don't know if that would be appropriate.
You're hemming my trousers—

FRANK

You're right.
It would be highly inappropriate.

> *They look at each other.*
> *Tilly's trousers fall down.*
> *They kiss.*
> *A tableau.*

6. Tilly Visits Lorenzo

Lorenzo interrupts the tableau.

LORENZO

So—you kissed this—Frank—while he was hemming your trousers.

TILLY

Yes.

LORENZO

I see. Did he kiss like an American? Were his lips hard? Did he move his tongue around like a tractor turning over the earth?

TILLY

Ah—no.

LORENZO

Did you hear music—inside your head—when you kissed him?

TILLY

No.

LORENZO

So it's nothing serious.

TILLY

Is the bank paying for this?

LORENZO

Tilly. I AM SUFFERING!
Look into my eyes.
Can you see the suffering?

TILLY

Yes.

Tilly helps Lorenzo onto the chaise.

LORENZO

Ever since I met you, there has been no morning and no evening.
There is only one long afternoon.
The afternoon is shaped like an almond.
Every day I think I will step into the almond like a boat
and ride it into evening.

But I lie down in the almond boat
and it is always afternoon.
I look up and there is no piazza—
there are no old men to play cards with
who know my family name.

TILLY

I understand, Lorenzo.

LORENZO

You do?

TILLY

I'll play cards with you.

LORENZO

Is that American for: I will be your bride?

TILLY

No.

Lorenzo moans quietly.

But I will play cards with you. And look out the window with you.
Then I have to get my hair cut.

LORENZO

You are cutting off your hair!

TILLY

Just a little bit.

LORENZO

No!

TILLY

Yes!

LORENZO

NO!

TILLY

YES!

LORENZO

Why?

TILLY

I need a trim.

LORENZO

But your hair—it is the sad song of a lark!

TILLY

Lorenzo. Be calm. It's just a trim. We will play cards. I am an old man. You are an old man. We live in Italy. We drink out of small cups. There is time for us to gaze out over the mountains and think about the past. You will think about your mother. I will think about my mother. But we will say nothing. We will play cards. Okay?

LORENZO

Will you save me the hair? From your haircut?

TILLY

Sure.

LORENZO

Can I touch your hair, before you go?

TILLY

Okay.

She lets him bury his face in her hair.

LORENZO

Oh! If only my whole being were just one big nose, to smell you always with.

A tableau.

7. Frances Cuts Tilly's Hair

Frances holds a mirror up to the back of Tilly's head.

FRANCES

You like it so far?

TILLY

Yes.

Frances cuts Tilly's hair some more.

I love this beauty shop.

FRANCES

Thank you.

TILLY

Is it all yours?

FRANCES

Yes, I own it.

TILLY

I walk past it every night, on the way home. I look in the window.
When it's all shut down, and the lights are off.

FRANCES

Really?

TILLY

Yes. At night—it's so beautiful—and empty, and sad.
All the hair is swept off the floor—as in: a woman has gone home
for the night.
There are plastic vestments draped on chairs
to catch the useless things that have fallen.

FRANCES

I'd never thought of it like that—

TILLY

There is a neon sign in the window—
it is in earnest about beautification.

FRANCES

You think my sign is earnest?

TILLY

In a good way.

FRANCES

It sounds like you've—thought about it.

TILLY

I have.

FRANCES

Your hair is incredibly healthy.

TILLY

I don't use conditioner. And I don't blow-dry it.

FRANCES

That's good. You should keep that up.

TILLY

Do women tell you lots of secrets when you cut their hair?

FRANCES

Stories you wouldn't believe.

TILLY

I thought so. Like what?

FRANCES

I can't tell.

TILLY

When I pass your beauty shop—at night—I imagine all the stories women have told during the day—holding court in green light. Stories with tiaras. And green wands. I'm sorry. Sometimes I get wound up. Then I tell people what I'm thinking.

FRANCES

So—what do you do?

TILLY

I work at a bank.

FRANCES

Really?

TILLY

Yes, why.

FRANCES

You don't seem like you work at a bank.

TILLY

What are you saying about banks?

FRANCES

Ah . . .

TILLY

Or—what are you saying about me?

FRANCES

I—

TILLY

You must have meant something by it.

FRANCES

Really, I didn't.

A pause. Tilly looks hurt.

Is anything wrong?

TILLY

No. I'm fine.

Frances finishes the haircut.

FRANCES

Well, I'm finished. Do you want to see?

TILLY

Oh no . . .

FRANCES

What's wrong?

TILLY

I hate for it to be over.

FRANCES

Well, I could comb it for five more minutes.

TILLY

That would be heaven.

FRANCES

Okay.

Frances combs Tilly's hair.

TILLY

Were you always a hairdresser?

FRANCES

No—a physicist.

TILLY

Really?

FRANCES

Yes.

TILLY

All those angles.

FRANCES

Yes.

TILLY

Then what?

FRANCES

I gave it up.

TILLY

Are you happier now?

FRANCES

Yes, I think so.

TILLY

That's good.

Frances combs Tilly's hair.

Do you ever feel melancholy, in the afternoon, sweeping up the hair that's no longer on anyone's head?

The stirring of music, played by Julian on his cello.
The lights dim.

FRANCES

Sometimes.

TILLY

I feel like I can smell the ocean.

FRANCES

I feel like I can smell the ocean, too!

TILLY

Right now?

FRANCES

Right now!

TILLY

Wow!

FRANCES

How about that?

TILLY

All the way from Illinois!

FRANCES

I can smell seaweed.

TILLY

I can smell salt.

FRANCES

Mmm.

TILLY

Are you from the ocean?

FRANCES

I used to live by the ocean.

TILLY

Oh—so you're far from home.
You're in—exile?

FRANCES

Well—I moved. From New Jersey.

TILLY

The wind is different by the ocean, isn't it?

FRANCES

I think so.

TILLY

Do you ever collect it—all that lost hair?

FRANCES

No. What would I use it for?

TILLY

Oh, nothing. So it wouldn't be left alone. So it would be with the other lost hair. Do you mind if I keep my hair?

FRANCES

No, that's fine.

TILLY

I love this time of afternoon.

FRANCES

Me, too.

TILLY

Me, too.

FRANCES

Me, too.

TILLY

Me, too.

FRANCES

Uh-oh.

SARAH RUHL

TILLY

What?

FRANCES

I have a nurse at home. She wouldn't like me to say "me too" three
times in a row.

TILLY

She takes care of you?

FRANCES

Well—kind of. I live with her.

TILLY

Oh. There's a word in Russian—it means melancholy—but not
exactly—it means to love someone but also to pity them.

FRANCES

You really do have beautiful hair.

Tilly and Frances look at each other.
Tilly puts her hand on Frances's cheek.
Tilly rips off her plastic haircutting vestment and hands it to Frances.
A brief tableau.

8. Lorenzo the Unfeeling from Behind a Window

As Tilly and Frances part:

LORENZO

Causes of Love Melancholy:
Temperature, Idleness, Diet.
Beauty from the Face,
Beauty from the Torso,
Beauty from the Eyes, and other parts.

Of all causes the remotest are stars.
Oh, Tilly. Why?

9. Frances Explains to Joan about Her Affair with Tilly

FRANCES

You're asking me—what she's like?

JOAN

Yes.

FRANCES

It won't make you feel funny if I tell you?

JOAN

I feel funny already.

FRANCES

What do you want to know about her?

JOAN

The usual things.

FRANCES

You're not going to get upset.

JOAN

No.

FRANCES

She's—delicate. She could spend an entire afternoon filling a bowl with water, and putting yellow flowers into the bowl.

JOAN

So—she's a hard worker.

FRANCES

Well . . . she's—tired—but in this—seductive way.

JOAN

I don't understand.

FRANCES

She makes her unhappiness into this sexy thing. She throws herself onto couches.

JOAN

You wanted to take care of her.

FRANCES

Yes—I did.

JOAN

She seemed—spontaneous.

FRANCES

Yes.

JOAN

With a name like "Tilly"—

FRANCES

Yes.

JOAN

Oh. I see.

FRANCES

I didn't want to upset you.

JOAN

I'm not upset. I'd like to meet her.

FRANCES

I don't know if that's a very good idea.

JOAN

We'll have tea. It will be civilized. I'm not a jealous person,
Frances. You know that.

10. Frank and Tilly

To the audience:

FRANK	TILLY
I took Tilly home to my apartment. I said:	I took Frank home to his apartment. He said:

FRANK

You are like—a painting—

TILLY

What painting?

FRANK

I don't know.
The one where a woman
looks sad and beautiful.

TILLY

Like this? *(A demonstration)*

FRANK

Yes.
Only—
your head goes over your shoulder,
a little to the left.
With your chin down.
And your eyes looking up.
Your eyes should look hopeful.
while your chin looks sad.

One thing goes up,
one thing goes down.
Yes.
Oh,
yes.
I wish I could paint you.

TILLY

Why don't you?

FRANK

I can't paint.

Frank and Tilly approach the audience.

FRANK	TILLY
Then we made love.	Then we made love.
Under the covers.	Under the covers.
The whole thing!	

TILLY

The room was dark,

FRANK

the sheets were damp,
it was everything I'd hoped for.

TILLY

And afterwards,

FRANK	TILLY
I held her in my arms.	I held him in my arms.
It was like a movie.	It was like a movie.
An aerial shot.	An aerial shot.
Her head on my chest.	His head on my chest.
Then she gazed up at me—	Then he gazed up at me—
I said:	he said:

FRANK

Play the seasick music.
I'm in love.

A pause. Julian begins to play lovelorn music. He stops.

TILLY

Wait—don't say that.

FRANK

Why?

TILLY

I'm scared.

FRANK

She said.
What are you scared of?
I asked.

TILLY

Have you ever seen what sadness looks like on a person, once they take off their gray shoes and gray gloves? It looks different. Not like a movie. People wear sweatpants when they are sad in private. Not pearls. You won't like it.

FRANK

That's not possible. Tilly. I love you.

FRANK AND TILLY

We breathed together in the dark for a long time.

FRANK

Then she began to cry.
She was beautiful when
she cried.

TILLY

Then I began to cry.
I'm beautiful when I cry.
I don't get in trouble with
policemen when I cry.

FRANK

Oh, Tilly.

TILLY

Oh, Frank.

FRANK

Oh, Tilly.

TILLY

Oh, Frank.

FRANK

Oh, God.

TILLY

God has no part in this.

FRANK

I'm sorry.
Oh, Tilly.

TILLY

Oh, Frank.

FRANK

Oh, Tilly.

TILLY

Wait—don't say my name again.

FRANK

What?

TILLY

Don't say it, I think.

FRANK

But I've been saying it.

TILLY

But now it's wrong.

FRANK

I don't understand.

TILLY

The first three times you said it right, the fifth time it felt—questionable—the sixth time wrong. That Tilly was not me.

FRANK

I said your name wrong?

TILLY

You *thought* my name wrong. You experienced a person who was not me. Then you spoke that person's name.

FRANK

I see.

TILLY

Try again.

FRANK

Tilly.

TILLY

No.

FRANK

Tilly.

TILLY

Closer.

FRANK

Tilly.

TILLY

Let's stop, Frank. Religious people don't address God directly in their prayers. They have a nickname for Him. So they don't get it wrong. That's why when you love someone you don't use their proper name. You call them something else. Like honey or spooky or shlumpy or little spoon. Do you understand me?

FRANK

Why are you so mean to me, Tilly?

TILLY

I don't know. Am I mean to you? I love you.

FRANK

You do?

TILLY

Yes.
Tell me something sad about your past. It will make us feel better. It will make us feel like we know each other.

FRANK

Okay, let me think.

A pause.
They turn toward the audience.

I told Tilly something sad
about my past.
Not the saddest thing, but fairly sad.

FRANK	TILLY
	I felt that I understood him.
We cried, at the same time.	We cried, at the same time.
I offered her my handkerchief.	

He gives her a handkerchief.

TILLY

You are the only man I have ever
met who still carries a
handkerchief!
I love you!

They embrace.

FRANK   TILLY

Tilly thought for three hours
about:
the lost Art   the lost Art
of the Handkerchief   of the Handkerchief
until she fell asleep.
I watched her sleep.
A strange desire came over me
to save her tears, forever.
I wrung out the handkerchief
into a little vial.
And I watched her sleep, all night.

11. Joan and Frances and Tilly Have Tea

Joan, Frances and Tilly sip their tea. Joan looks Tilly over.

JOAN

Would you like some more *hot water?*

TILLY

No thank you.

FRANCES

Would anyone care for a little tea sandwich shaped like a triangle?

TILLY

I like triangles.

FRANCES

Good, then. Joan, pass the triangle-shaped sandwiches.

JOAN

Certainly.

TILLY

MMM!—this triangle-shaped tea sandwich is good.
What—
is on it?

FRANCES

Canned asparagus and mayonnaise. It's a real treat in New Zealand.

TILLY

I've never been to New Zealand.

JOAN

I've never been to New Zealand either. Out of the three of us,
only Frances has been to New Zealand. That means we have something in common, Tilly.

TILLY

More than one thing, I would imagine, Joan.

FRANCES

It's lovely weather we're having.

TILLY

Unseasonably warm.

JOAN

You're just a young thing, aren't you?

TILLY

I'm fairly young—yes.

JOAN

I think that's wonderful, to be young.

TILLY

I'm sad most of the time.

JOAN

But it's wonderful to be young.

TILLY

Yes—you're right—it is wonderful.

JOAN

Don't get old.

TILLY

You're hardly old. My goodness.

JOAN

You have beautiful eyes. Doesn't she, Frances?

TILLY

You do, too.

JOAN

Do you think so? Really?

TILLY

Yes.

JOAN

No.

TILLY

Oh, yes. Here—let me look.

Tilly approaches Joan's face and looks into her eyes.

You have orange rings around the pupils—

JOAN

Frances—I have orange rings in my eyes!

FRANCES

I heard.

JOAN

Don't you think that's marvelous?

FRANCES

Yes, Joan.

JOAN

Frances, close your eyes and tell me what color my eyes are.

FRANCES

I know what color your eyes are.

JOAN

She sounds testy, doesn't she?

TILLY

Are you upset, Frances?

JOAN

She gets this way.

FRANCES

I love to be talked about in the third person.

JOAN

She hates to be talked about in the third person.

TILLY

It's such a beautiful dining room you have.

JOAN   FRANCES
Thank you.   Thank you.

TILLY

The wallpaper is so gorgeous.

JOAN

Until I met Frances, I hated wallpaper.

TILLY

Really? Why?

JOAN

It reminded me of covered-up things. Bloodstains.

TILLY

Of course—

JOAN

Girls who wear pearls. White-and-blue floral patterns.

TILLY

Yes—I can see that.

JOAN

But Frances grew up with wallpaper. She likes it. Don't you, Frances?

FRANCES

You're so talkative today, Joan.
She's usually shy.

JOAN

That's true. I'm a very shy person.

TILLY

I think that's nice. To be shy.

JOAN

Thank you.

TILLY

I think it's interesting when a shy person says, "I'm a shy person."
Because it's not a very shy thing to say.

JOAN

That's true. I hadn't thought of that.

TILLY

Or when a person says, "I'm not a self-absorbed person." Isn't it funny when someone says that? Because they're—you know— talking about themselves?

Joan and Frances laugh.

Or when someone says, "Do you think I'm insecure?" Do you get it—because if they have to ask—

Joan and Frances laugh.

I always find that funny. When people say those things.

Pause.

I'm dating a man named Frank now. He's a tailor.

FRANCES

Frank?

TILLY

Yes—Frank. Isn't that a beautiful name? Like Frankfurter. Sort of American. I love the smell of hot dogs. At a baseball game.

Pause. Joan and Frances look at Tilly.

Do you ever have the feeling, when you wake up in the morning, that you're in love but you don't know with what?

JOAN	FRANCES
Yes!	Yes!

Joan and Frances look at each other, irritated.

TILLY

It's this feeling that you want to love strangers, that you want to
kiss the man at the post office, or the woman at the dry cleaners—
you want to wrap your arms around life, life itself, but you can't,
and this feeling wells up in you, and there is nowhere to put this
great happiness—and you're floating—and then you fall down
and become unbearably sad. And you have to go lie down on the
couch.

JOAN   FRANCES

I know what you mean.   Are you still in therapy, Tilly?

Joan and Frances look at each other, irritated.

FRANCES

Are you still in therapy?

TILLY

That's funny. Everyone is always asking me: Tilly, are you still in
therapy? I say something like: I had a bad day. And they say: Tilly,
are you still in therapy? I go to therapy and my therapist falls in
love with me. I have to be careful.

JOAN

How so?

Tilly moves toward the audience.
Her speech becomes a public speech.
Stirring music from Julian.

TILLY

I'm not particularly smart.
I'm not particularly beautiful.
But I suffer so well, and so often.
A stranger sees me cry—
and they see a river they haven't
swum in—

a river in a foreign country—
so they take off their trousers
and jump in the water.
They take pictures
with a waterproof camera,
they dry themselves in the sun.
They're all dry
and I'm still wet.
Maybe my suffering is from another time.
A time when suffering was sexy.
When the afternoons, and the streets,
were full of rain.
Maybe my tears don't come from this century.
Maybe I inherited them from old well water.

The music stops.

Wait.
Am I acting weird?

JOAN AND FRANCES

No, no.

TILLY

I'm sorry. Do you mind if I lie on your couch for a moment?
I'm feeling sort of—

She feels melancholy.

JOAN AND FRANCES

Please do.

Tilly lies down on their couch. Joan and Frances look at her.
They stroke Tilly's hair.

TILLY

Should I be making small talk?

JOAN

No—no, don't bother with that.

TILLY

All right.
Will you both smile for a moment?

They both smile.

You both have very nice teeth. Have you had dental work?

JOAN   FRANCES
No.   Yes.

TILLY

They don't have dental work in England, do they?

JOAN

No, they don't.

TILLY

I like bad teeth. So you look old when you're old, like you're supposed to.

JOAN

Yes.

TILLY

Maybe you could put on some music.

JOAN

What would you like to hear?

TILLY

Oh, anything.

*Joan exits to put on a record,
perhaps late 1960s French.*

Frances mounts Tilly.
Joan returns.
Frances unmounts Tilly.

I love this album.
I'm suddenly tired. I think I'd better go now. Thank you for the
New Zealand sandwiches. They were delicious. And it was so nice
to meet you, Joan. Frances has told me a great deal about you. And
it's all true.

JOAN

I'll show you to the door.
Good-bye.

TILLY

Good-bye.

FRANCES

Good-bye!

Tilly exits.
Joan looks after her as she goes.
Frances shuts the door.

So.

JOAN

So.

FRANCES

Now you know.

JOAN

Now I know.

FRANCES

And?

JOAN

It's strange, Frances. But I have this sexy sad feeling I've never had before. Like I'm in a European city before the war. We must invite her over again. Not for lunch. For dinner.

Let's open a window. It's hot in here.

FRANCES

Joan—I'm the one who was supposed to be having the affair. Me.

JOAN

I'm going to open a window.

She opens a window.

She has this remarkable smell—like old perfume—those little glass bottles with red thingmabobs that you squeeze like this—

Joan pretends to put perfume on her neck.

FRANCES

My mouth feels dry.

JOAN

In what way?

FRANCES

Like after you eat an almond. And before you want to kiss someone.

Joan moves in to kiss Frances.

Joan.

JOAN

What is it?

FRANCES

Let me smell your hair.

JOAN

Okay.

FRANCES

I can't smell it.

JOAN

What?

FRANCES

I can't smell it. Did you switch shampoos?

JOAN

No.

FRANCES

My God, Joan, I think I've lost my sense of smell.

JOAN

You're probably congested.
Here—smell my skin.

She does.

FRANCES

Nothing.

JOAN

Nothing? That's strange.

FRANCES

Nothing.

Joan and Frances look at each other.

1 2 . Tilly, Alone

TILLY

Tonight I'm older than all the books.
I'm older than all the bricks in all the courtyards.
And I could write the saddest songs.
I want Frank.
I miss Frank.
I haven't seen Frank in two hours.
I wish I lived in a time when
people went to sea for years on end.
When there were still countries to be discovered.
I wish I could go on a ship for three years disguised as a boy.
I wish I were there right now,
writing a long letter to Frank by candlelight.
I wish there was salt wind in my hair.

A church bell rings midnight.

It's my birthday.

Frank appears with flowers.

FRANK

Happy birthday.

TILLY

I was longing for you—and you appeared.

FRANK

Happy birthday, Tilly.

TILLY

Frank. I'm overwhelmed. You've made me very happy.

FRANK

I did?

TILLY

Yes!
You said happy birthday. It's my birthday. And I'm happy.
The way you're supposed to be on your birthday.
I feel like singing.

Julian plucks happy chords on his cello.
Everyone enters.

13. A Song

TILLY

I'm happy.
I'm happy.
Happy birthday.
I'm happy.

FRANK

Happiness is buck-toothed.
Happiness is bleeding.
Happiness wears
gold-capped teeth.

LORENZO

I was abandoned at a candy shop

JOAN

There's a word for it——

FRANCES

There's a word for it——

TILLY	JOAN
Remember?	Remember?
Remember?	Remember?

ALL

But not in English!
Not in English!

TILLY	FRANCES
I smelled the ocean . . .	I smelled the ocean . . .

FRANK

What kind of a name is Frank . . .

JOAN

It's not really practical . . .

ALL	TILLY
All these windows!	Happy birthday!
All these windows!	Happy birthday!
All these windows!	Happy birthday to me!

14. Tilly Becomes Happy

Joan, Frances, Tilly and Lorenzo.

TILLY

I wanted to invite everyone I love to my birthday party.
Thank you all for coming.
Frank couldn't come. He has a stomach ache.
Would anyone care for an almond?

She passes almonds around in a little dish. Everyone eats one.

What shall we play?
Frances—do you have an idea?

FRANCES

No.

JOAN

We could play duck-duck-goose.

TILLY

Oh, yes, oh, yes, let's play duck-duck-goose!!! Joan, you be it.
Everyone sit in a circle.

LORENZO

I don't know your duck-duck-goose.

JOAN

Duck.
Duck.
Duck . . .
Goose!

Joan tags Lorenzo.
Lorenzo stands, not knowing what to do.
Joan runs around the circle and sits in his spot.

TILLY

Lorenzo: you lost. That means you're "it."
Tap us on the head.

Lorenzo, tapping Frances, then Joan:

LORENZO

Person.
Person . . .

JOAN

It's duck-duck-goose.
You say: duck-duck-goose.

LORENZO

I will play it my way.
Person . . . *(Tapping Joan)*
Person . . . *(Tapping Frances)*
Goddess! *(Tags Tilly)*

Tilly chases Lorenzo.
He tries to slow down so that he can turn around and kiss her.

TILLY

No, Lorenzo, run, run!

LORENZO

I love you!

JOAN

He goes in the mush-pot.

TILLY

That's right, Lorenzo. You'll have to go in the mush-pot.

LORENZO

I will not go in a mush-pot.

TILLY

Then run!

Lorenzo doesn't move.
Tilly chases him.
He moves backward, unwilling, to his spot.

Now sit.

Lorenzo sits in his spot.
Tilly is "it."
She looks around at the group.

I can hardly play.
I'm so overcome by emotion
having all the people
I love in one room together.
Well, except for Frank.
I wish Frank were here too.
Let's make a little pretend spot for Frank.

Joan and Frances move to make a little pretend spot for Frank.

Okay.
Duck.
Duck.
Duck . . .
I just want to go on like this forever. I want it never to end.

Tilly taps each on the head.
She is overwhelmed by their beauty.
This makes her happy.

Duck.
Duck.
Duck.
Duck . . .
I can't choose.
Duck.
Duck . . .
You're all so beautiful. I can't stand it.
Duck . . .
Life really does have moments of transcendent beauty, doesn't it?
At a party—each face—a flower—each face a—
Duck.
Duck . . .
I'm so happy—
Duck . . .
I'm so happy—

FRANCES

Are you all right, Tilly?

TILLY

I'm so happy—I don't know what to do . . . I'm sorry. I'm going
to go in the other room to lie down. Joan, you be it.

Tilly exits. Joan gets up. They all look at each other.
Strange exultant music.
An intermission, or not. Preferably not.

PART 2

1. The Consequence of Tilly's Great Happiness

Frank looks out the window.
Tilly enters at full speed.

TILLY

Frank!

FRANK

What's wrong, Tilly? You look weird.

TILLY

I just had my birthday party. And Frank—I feel happy.

FRANK

Really?

TILLY

Yes. I feel—light. Giddy.

FRANK

You do?

TILLY

Yes. Frank—I think you've made me happy.

FRANK

But I wasn't at the party.

TILLY

Yes, I feel happy. I really do. How do you feel?

FRANK

I don't know.

TILLY

You look funny.

FRANK

I'm just—adjusting. To your being—happy.

TILLY

I feel—positively cheerful.

FRANK

Really—cheerful.

TILLY

My God, this is strange, I'm starting to feel happier, and happier,
and happier—has my face changed—

She looks in the mirror.
She touches her face.

Do I look different?—I feel—oh God, I feel—kiss me Frank—

FRANK

In a minute—

TILLY

Kiss me now—I want to share my great happiness with you—

FRANK

I don't feel—sexually aroused—at this juncture.

TILLY

Why, Frank?

FRANK

You look different.

TILLY

I'm happy!

FRANK

Yes.

TILLY

Don't you want me to be happy?

FRANK

I—

TILLY

Let's dance!

FRANK

I have a stomach ache.

TILLY

Frank?
Frank . . .

She does a small dance of hopping toward him.

FRANK

You're saying my name wrong.
That Frank was not me.

Tilly.
I feel your happiness coming on like a great big storm.

TILLY

A storm?

FRANK

Your eyes aren't looking at me. They're looking at a great big storm
of happiness. On the horizon.
Can you see me?

He waves his hand in front of her face.

TILLY

I think I need to be alone with my happiness.
Or else with crowds of people in a public square.
Maybe I'll go to the bank and do some extra work.
Good-bye.

2 . Tilly Confesses Her Happiness to Lorenzo

Lorenzo eating marzipan.
Tilly enters.

TILLY

I wanted to tell you first. I'm happy.

LORENZO

What?

TILLY

Happy.

LORENZO

You have to admit this comes as something of a shock.

TILLY

I'm so sorry.

LORENZO

Happy?

TILLY

Happy.

LORENZO

No *trace*?
Every drop—*gone*?

TILLY

No trace.
I'm in love again.
Not with Frank.
With a woman who writes obituaries.
She has such a positive attitude.
I met her at the bank.
She was withdrawing all her money.
All of it.
Carpe diem, she said.
That's right, I said.
She said: you really seem to enjoy your work.
I said: I do.
She said: I like that.
We wake up at six A.M. and go biking
before she finds out who's dead.
She writes the greatest obituaries.
They're not like the regular ones—
they've got flair.
They're like little poems.
My God!
I am *so* happy.

LORENZO

We can do a blood test . . .

TILLY

I don't need a blood test.
I'm happy.

LORENZO

Let's look out the window.

He grabs her hand.
They look out the window. He directs her gaze.
Sad music from Julian.

Look at that old woman, walking home from the store by herself.
For whom is she buying that gallon of milk? Where is her husband?
It will be too much milk for her—she will think of her husband
who is dead from the war. How much of the milk will sit, unused,
in the afternoon, while she drinks her solitary cup of tea?

TILLY

The woman is sad. And beautiful. And she makes me happy.

LORENZO

Don't do this to me.

TILLY

I'm sorry. I told the bank I was happy and they won't pay for any
more sessions.
I'm cured.
Oh—here is the hair from my haircut.
I saved it.
For you.
A relic from another time.
Enjoy it.

She hands him a small packet of hair.
A tableau.

3. Frank Continues His Defense

Frank, to the audience:

FRANK

I want to present to you, this evening—a defense of melancholy.
Stars a cause.
Love a cause.
Death a cause.
Tilly—a main cause.

4. Joan and Frances and Tilly

Frances in her pajamas. Joan in her nurse's uniform.
Tilly appears on her bicycle.

TILLY

Hello! Thought I'd stop by! I'm on a very long bike ride!

JOAN AND FRANCES

Hello.

TILLY

I wanted to tell you both. I'm happy.

FRANCES

Yes, you look—happy.

TILLY

I still love you both but in a happy way. I want to throw dinner parties and go hiking and plant nasturtiums. It's such a beautiful day
out. Why are you both indoors on a day like this? Frances, you
look terrible. What's wrong?

FRANCES

Nothing.

TILLY

Well . . . call me if you want to go biking!
I can loan you my ten-speed!

Tilly exits.
Frances lies down on the ground.

FRANCES

My God.

JOAN

Well, I'm happy that she's happy.

FRANCES

She's not happy. She's monstrous.

JOAN

Well. No use crying over spilt milk. You should go to work.

FRANCES

I should go to work.
You should go to work.
I'm taking a melancholy day.

JOAN

There's no such thing, is there?

FRANCES

There is when you own your own hair salon.

JOAN

I don't feel like going to work either.

JOAN AND FRANCES

Let's stay home.

FRANCES

Let's lie down.

JOAN

Yes, let's.

They lie down in each other's arms.

FRANCES

I can't smell anything.

JOAN

Still?

FRANCES

I had my morning coffee this morning
and I couldn't smell it.
It was like a commercial—
you know how in a commercial
you can see the people nodding and smiling
and smelling their coffee,
but you can't smell what's on TV?

JOAN

Do you have a sinus infection?

FRANCES

No.
Maybe the rest of my life will be like television.
No smell.

Frances unravels. The following is not a reflective meditation.

Joan.
Have you ever noticed
that if you *listen* to something,
then you *hear* it
and that *thing* you *hear*
is a *sound*?

JOAN

Yes.

FRANCES

Okay. That's three different things! Listening, hearing, and the thing you hear. Three things. But if you try to *smell* something then you can *smell* it and what you *smell* is a *smell*. They could only come up with *one* word for it.

JOAN

Huh.

FRANCES

I mean—*why* do you think that is?

JOAN

I don't know.

FRANCES

Joan—my skin is dry.
Why is my skin so dry?
It's like bark.

JOAN

You're right. I'll put some lotion on it.
I'm going to call in sick.

She moves to call in sick. She stops.

Wait.
I can't call in sick.
I'm a nurse.
People need me.
There's a man dying on the seventh floor.

FRANCES

I need you.

JOAN

I'm going to work now, Frances.
I'll ask a doctor about your smell problem.

Why don't you rake some leaves or shovel some snow or something like that?

FRANCES

I don't have a shovel.
It's springtime.

JOAN

Cheer up, Frances.

FRANCES

Cheer up?

JOAN

I'll call you from work.
I love you, Frances.

FRANCES

Please, Joan. I have a bad feeling. I can't smell anything.
How will I know if the house is burning down?

JOAN

You're not being rational.

FRANCES

I hate rational.

JOAN

You're a physicist.

FRANCES

Was! Was!

JOAN

Honestly, Frances, you're being a child!

FRANCES

Oh, go take care of sick people. I know how much you like to do
that. Good-bye.

JOAN

Good-bye.

Joan exits.
Frances sits up.
Frank appears in another window.
To the audience:

FRANCES	FRANK
I would like to curl up and become a small thing. About this big.	I would like to curl up and become a small thing. About this big.

They pinch their fingers together—half an inch.

And still. Very still. Have you ever been so melancholy, that you wanted to fit in the palm of your beloved's hand? And lie there, for fortnights, or decades, or the length of time in between stars? In complete silence? Shhh. *(A finger to the lips)*	And still. Very still. Have you ever been so melancholy, that you wanted to fit in the palm of your beloved's hand? And lie there, for fortnights, or decades, or the length of time in between stars? In complete silence? Shhh. *(A finger to the lips)*

Frances walks to a window and looks out.
Frank goes to see a therapist.

5. Frank Goes to See Lorenzo the Unfeeling

LORENZO

Go on.

FRANK

I was hemming her pants, and I fell in love.

LORENZO

I know what love is!

FRANK

Excuse me?

LORENZO

Go on, go on.

Lorenzo is distracted.
He eats marzipan.

FRANK

She was so beautiful—when she was sad—I couldn't help myself—
I wanted to bathe in her sadness like a bath—

LORENZO

Of course you did.

FRANK

She would cry sometimes in her sleep.
I put her tears in a little vial. I collected them.

LORENZO

Ah, like the Romans.

FRANK

What?

LORENZO

The Romans. Collected tears in little vials. Buried them with the
dead.

FRANK

This vial is all I have left of her. Is that weird?

Frank produces a vial of tears.

LORENZO

Yes, it is weird. Would you like some candy? Marzipan. It's good.

FRANK

No, thank you. But you said the Romans did it.

LORENZO

Forget the Romans. Go on.

Lorenzo eats marzipan.

FRANK

I never loved someone so much. Now—she's gone—and I wish I were dead.

Lorenzo laughs.

FRANK

Why are you laughing?

LORENZO

Perhaps I am laughing because, I, too, have felt the way that you feel, Frank.

FRANK

Oh.

LORENZO

You seem—depressed.

FRANK

Maybe a little.

LORENZO

It is my medical opinion that you should go on medication. It's a very good medication. It will make you feel—very nice.

FRANK

I am sad because I fell out of love. I am not sad like: "I want to take medication."

LORENZO

Frank. Maybe you should have a little stay at the hospital.

FRANK

I don't want to stay at a hospital! I think I will move to another country. In French movies, people *die* of love. They *die* of it.

LORENZO

Frank. Frank. Poor Frank. Why don't you continue with your story.

FRANK

Well—one day—all at once—with no explanation—she was— happy. Cheerful, even. It was like a violent accident. A car wreck. We suddenly had nothing in common. I felt—so far away from her. Her face got red when she was happy, like a sweaty cow. And her voice got louder. And her eyes got glazed over, like a sweaty cow.

LORENZO

Yes! And how did that make you feel?

FRANK

Well, Tilly came home from her birthday party—

LORENZO

Tilly?

FRANK

That's the woman's name. Tilly.

LORENZO

I was at Tilly's birthday party! Not you!

FRANK

You know Tilly?

LORENZO

Do I know Tilly?
DO I KNOW TILLY!

FRANK

This is outrageous. *I* am paying *YOU*!

LORENZO

Give me that vial of tears.

FRANK

No!

LORENZO

Give it here!

FRANK

No! It's mine! It's mine! I collected them!

LORENZO

Her tears belong to me!

Stirring fight music, from Julian.
Frank and Lorenzo wrestle over the vial of tears.
This wrestling goes on for a good minute,
with much swearing, name-calling,
and knocking over of furniture.
Joan appears at the door.
She knocks.

JOAN

(From outside) Is anything wrong?

She hears scuffling.

FRANK

Bastard!

LORENZO

Imbecile! Give it!

Joan enters.

JOAN

What's going on?

*Lorenzo wrestles Frank to the ground
and sits astride him.*

LORENZO

Give me the vial or I will drool onto your face!

FRANK

I won't give it!

JOAN

(Over the shouting) Lorenzo? Are you a doctor?
Who is the doctor and who is the patient?

LORENZO

I am now going to let saliva drop down from my mouth—if you
give me the vial, I will suck the drool back up—now—now!

FRANK

I won't! I won't!

JOAN

Should I call security?

LORENZO

Leave me alone with my patient, please.
Give me the vial, Frank. Give it up.

FRANK

Her tears are mine!

LORENZO

I'm going to drool!

FRANK

(To Joan) I don't know who you are—but please—help me—take this vial—and run! Run! It belongs to a woman named Tilly—

> *Frank reaches out toward Joan.*
> *Lorenzo pulls on Frank's legs.*
> *Joan takes the vial.*
> *She looks at the audience.*
> *A tableau.*
> *Strange music, from Julian, on his cello*

6. The Vial of Tears

Frances, staring out the window.
Joan, holding the vial of tears, walks toward Frances.

FRANCES

What's that?

JOAN

Tilly's tears.

FRANCES

Give it.

JOAN

Why?

> *Joan gives Frances the vial.*
> *Frances drinks the tears.*

Frances! Honestly!!!

Joan and Frances look at each other.
Joan holds out her hand for the vial.
Music from Julian.

7. A Song from the Company

The music from Julian continues.
Joan, Frances, Frank and Lorenzo appear.

JOAN, FRANCES, FRANK AND LORENZO

Oh, for the melancholy Tilly!
Why did she become so silly?
We loved her when she had
The capacity for pity!
Oh, for the melancholy Tilly!

JOAN AND FRANCES	FRANK AND LORENZO
Stars a cause	Junk food a cause
Love a cause	Cheetos and Doritos
Death a cause	And cheddar Goldfish a cause.
Oh, for the melancholy Tilly!	Oh, for the melancholy Tilly!

JOAN, FRANCES, FRANK AND LORENZO

Life used to be so slow
Life used to be so sweet
Life used to be banisters
And rain-drenched cobbled streets!
Oh, for the melancholy Tilly!

JOAN AND FRANCES	FRANK AND LORENZO
Stars a cause	Narrow streets
Love a cause	And telegrams
Death a cause	And cheddar Goldfish a cause.
Oh, for the melancholy Tilly!	

Tilly walks across the stage holding a helium balloon.
They look at her.

JOAN, FRANCES, FRANK AND LORENZO

Life used to be so slow
Life used to be so sweet
Life used to be balconies
And paintings by Magritte!
Oh, for the melancholy Tilly!
Oh, for the melancholy Tilly!

The song ends.
A tableau. A suspended moment.
Frances looks at everyone.
The light changes.
Frances has a revelation.
Lights glow on Frances.
She has a desire to disappear.

FRANCES

Oh!

Frances rides on a window out through a door,
or walks through a balcony,
or she makes a very long cross.
Whatever it is—
she does something melancholy, slow and theatrical.
Full of longing, mysterious, simple, riveting.
She slows down time for us.
She makes us wonder.
This only lasts about six seconds.
We watch her.

8. Joan Reveals a Terrible Secret to Tilly

Joan and Tilly are at a café.
Tilly drinks a Coke with a straw.
Joan wears dark glasses and a scarf.

TILLY

And I continue to get happier and happier and happier. It's like a sickness. No one likes to hear about it. A brick could fall on my head and it would somehow increase my pleasure. Joan—is something wrong?

JOAN

Well, yes.

TILLY

Oh, I'm sorry. I've been so self-absorbed. What is it?

JOAN

It's Frances.

TILLY

Is something wrong with Frances? Is she ill?

JOAN

Not exactly.

TILLY

What is it?

JOAN

It's—she's—she's turned into an almond.

Pause.

TILLY

What?

JOAN

It's the oddest thing. I came home from work. When I left she was lying on the couch, looking out the window. When I came back, there was an almond on the pillow.

TILLY

No!

JOAN

Yes.

TILLY

I'm so sorry.

JOAN

I feel terrible. She told me not to go to work that day. She'd lost her sense of smell. But I went to work. I left her.

TILLY

It's not your fault, Joan. You can't blame yourself for this.

JOAN

She lies in bed, so still, so quiet—so oval-shaped. She looks like she's about to cough, but she can't, because she's an almond.

TILLY

Can I see her?

JOAN

Of course.

9. By the Bedside of Frances the Almond

Joan enters, carrying a small white pillow,
upon which is laid an almond.
Joan puts down the pillow.
Tilly kneels beside the almond.

TILLY

Oh, Frances. Is it my fault? Have I brought you to this? Don't speak, Frances.

JOAN

Any sign?

TILLY

No.

Tilly pets the almond.

I can't help but feel that this is somehow my fault.
Do you have any salt, Joan?

JOAN

I'll get some.

TILLY

I'll salt you, Frances. That will make you feel better. Salted almonds
are so much better than plain ones.

Joan enters with salt.
Tilly puts some salt on Frances the almond.

How does that feel?
You're beautiful, Frances.
(To Joan, in a whisper) Are you sure this is Frances?

JOAN

It seems like Frances, doesn't it?

TILLY

Yes.
I'm so sorry, Joan.
Talk to me, Frances.
It's Tilly.
Are you all right in there?
So quiet.
So quiet.
What are you thinking about, Frances?
Frances?
I love you.
Frances!
How do you talk to an almond?

She tosses the almond up in the air three times.

Whee!
Whee!
Wasn't that fun, Frances?
You're so little now.
And so light.
The good news is that I'm happy, Frances.
Everyone around me seems so sad
and I just can't relate.
I feel like a little red sports car.
Can you hear me, Frances?
Give me a sign.
Come on, Frances.

She listens to the almond.

Joan—what reason do you have to believe that Frances actually turned *into* an almond? I mean—is it possible—that she ran away, and put an almond on the chair—as a kind of—going-away present? Like a mint—at a hotel?

JOAN

She wouldn't leave me.

TILLY

I'm going to taste her.

Joan is shocked.
Tilly licks Frances the almond.

It tastes—sort of like Frances. I don't know—if Frances were an almond is this how she would taste? About like this?

Tilly licks the almond again.

(Puzzled) Is it—familiar? I don't know.

JOAN

I haven't called the police yet.

TILLY

Much better to leave them out of this, I think.

They regard the almond.
They blow on the almond.
They knock on the almond.

JOAN

Maybe we should eat her.

TILLY

No!

JOAN

She would want it that way. To become a part of us. She can't
think! She can't feel!
She's not even—a vegetable! She's—she's a nut, Tilly.

TILLY

Joan—do you think there are others—like Frances?

A letter is shoved under a door.

JOAN

What is it?

TILLY

A letter.

JOAN

Read it.

The music of intrigue, from Julian, on his cello.

TILLY

If you are experiencing any form of melancholy: stay in your home. I repeat: STAY IN YOUR HOME. Occupy your mind. Occupy your hands. Do not look out the window in the afternoon dreaming of the past or far-off things or absent people or dead people or the sea. People experiencing melancholy have been turning into almonds on the street.

Do not eat these almonds. Do not step on these almonds. If you *do* find an almond, or if a family member *becomes* an almond, *do* put him or her in a zip-lock bag and deposit it in the nearest mailbox.

JOAN

Who's it from?

TILLY

Anonymous.

Tilly and Joan turn and look at each other, frightened.
They look at the almond.
A thin beam of light on the almond.

10. Inside the Almond

Frances appears in a well of light, behind a window.
To the audience:

FRANCES

It's nice in here.
It's quiet.

11. Lorenzo

Lorenzo, walking down the street,
stepping on almonds.
To the audience:

It is—an epidemic!
The streets are littered—
littered—with almonds!
I stepped on one—
I stepped on two—
on my way here.
I crushed them
under my shoe.
See?

1 2. Joan at Work, the Night Shift

Joan takes Frances out of her pocket.

JOAN

Hi, Frances.
I miss you, Frances.
Everything is going to be all right, Frances. I promise you.
I'm a nurse. I can fix things.
Now . . .
Let's see.

Cures for melancholy:
Food a remedy.
Music a remedy.
Love—a remedy.
Okay.

Causes of melancholy:
Food a cause.
Music a cause.
Love—a cause.

Well. That's a problem.

13. Tilly Goes to Frank's Tailor Shop

TILLY

Frank. I had to see you.

FRANK

I'm busy. I'm sewing.

TILLY

I know you don't want to see me.
But I'm in trouble, Frank.
My friend—has turned into an almond.
And I'm afraid that it's my fault.

FRANK

What?

TILLY

And meanwhile, I feel lighter and lighter.
I am trying to cultivate—a sensation of—gravity.
But nothing helps.

FRANK

An almond?

TILLY

Yes.
Frank—you can fix most things.
If a jacket doesn't fit—you can fix it.
If a dress has a hole—you can mend it.
How can I fix Frances?

FRANK

Frances?

TILLY

Yes, Frances.
Frank, you've turned pale.

FRANK

Tilly—there is something I have never told you because the memory was too painful. I was separated at birth from my twin sister—Frances.

Stirring music from Julian.

We were abandoned at a toy store in an unspecified Scandinavian country. My mother—melancholy by nature—sailed the fjords and never came back. My father—a toy maker—longed to follow her. And so he hid us in large gift-wrapped packages and stowed us away on ships, bound for America.

Do you know the pain of being gift-wrapped at a young age? My first memory is of being opened.

My sister—Frances was her name—was shipped to New Jersey. And I was sent to Illinois. But all my life, I have been haunted—longing for my lost Scandinavian sister, Frances.

TILLY

My God!
You look exactly like her!

FRANK

So it's true.

TILLY

Why didn't you tell me sooner?
Now it's too late.

FRANK

My sister—has turned into—an almond?

TILLY

I'm afraid so.

FRANK

How did this happen?

Frances appears in a well of light behind a window.

FRANCES

Because the quiet was all she owned,
she walked to an almond tree,
undid the branches . . .
and lying down
became an almond.

She disappears.

TILLY

We have to get her back.
How do you get to where almonds are?
Can you climb a tree?
Can you sail there?

FRANK

Let me think.

TILLY

There's a word—in another language—it means—to be so
melancholy that you turn into an inanimate object.

FRANK

What is the word?

TILLY

I don't know.

FRANK

What is the language?

TILLY

A dead language, I think.

FRANK

Don't worry. We'll find her.

TILLY

Oh, Frank.
I've missed you.

They embrace.
Tilly weeps tears into Frank's suit.

FRANK

Tilly? Are you crying?

TILLY

Yes.

FRANK

We have to collect your tears.

TILLY

What?

14. Joan, Tilly, Frank, Lorenzo and Frances the Almond

TILLY

We're all here with a common purpose.
To get Frances back.

LORENZO

(To Frank) You again.

FRANK

Let's be friends, Lorenzo, for the sake of Frances.
(Turning toward the almond) This is my sister?

JOAN

I'm afraid so.

FRANK

Can I hold her?

JOAN

Of course.

Joan hands Frank the almond.

FRANK

Frances!

TILLY

Do you recognize her?

FRANK

I think so.

JOAN

Frances.
I'd rather be an almond with you
than be a person with me.
Tell me how to be an almond.
Tell me, tell me, tell me.
I'll be quiet.

TILLY

Can you hear anything?

JOAN

No.
I'm sorry I told you to cheer up, Frances.
That was stupid.

A moment of respect for Joan's loss.

FRANK

Tilly, I believe you have the vial of tears.

TILLY

Frank has an idea.

FRANK

If we each drink one sip from the vial of tears, we will become almonds, and we will find Frances.

LORENZO

I don't want to be an almond. I like my body!

Tilly stands on a chair.
She delivers a rousing speech.

TILLY

Lorenzo. When someone in your social circle becomes so melancholy that they stop moving, it is your duty as a human being to *go find them*. It is not enough to seek medical attention. It is not enough to ask them how they are feeling. You must go where they are and *get* them. It is up to *all of us* to save Frances. It is part of the social contract.

JOAN, FRANK AND LORENZO

It is?

TILLY

It should be!

LORENZO

I go where Tilly goes.

FRANK

Okay, then.
We'll put Frances in the center of the circle.

They put Frances in the center of the circle.
They each drink from the vial of tears.
They all hold hands. They shut their eyes.
The lights fade to blackness for the first and only time in the play.
An extended note on the cello.
A chant in the dark—somewhere between a madrigal and a liturgical chant:

JOAN, TILLY, FRANK AND LORENZO

Cellos and the color blue. Olives.
Vespers. Rain in the middle of a tree branch.

Windows. The sound of crickets,
memories of an unseen lighthouse.
A broken fence, a broken onion,
lost objects, windows, dust,
hallways with a particular smell
which you will never revisit,
most forms of longing,
windows, wind, windows.

The lights go up.
Frances has appeared in the center of the circle.
Everyone gasps.

FRANCES

Am I in the mush-pot?
Is this duck-duck-goose?

JOAN

Frances!

FRANCES

Joan!

TILLY

Frances!

FRANCES

Tilly!

FRANK

Frances! It's Frank, your long-lost brother.

FRANCES

Frank, my long-lost brother!

Frank and Frances embrace.

Where did you——? How did you——?

FRANK

All my life—
Something missing.

When you were a child did you
look out the window at the moon—

at the very same time—
only in New Jersey?
Yes.

FRANCES

All my life—
Something missing.

Yes—and wonder
if you were looking
out the window at the moon
at the very same time—
only in Illinois?
Yes.

FRANCES

My God!
Frank!

FRANK

Frances!

LORENZO

Wait—
a moment—
a moment—
are we—all of us—now almonds?

FRANK

How could we know?

JOAN

How could we know?

FRANK

Is this how an almond looks to another almond?

They look at one another.
They rush to a mirror.
They look in the mirror for a good long while.

TILLY

Did Frances come to us or did we come to Frances?
Frances?

FRANCES

I don't know.

JOAN

Perhaps it's best not to know.

FRANCES

(To Joan) Did you love me, Joan, when I went into a deep well of
silence?

JOAN

Yes.

> *A silence. Then, stirring music from Julian.*
> *They all hear the music, for the first time.*
> *This makes them happy.*

TILLY

Someone's playing music!

> *They all notice Julian, for the first time.*

(To Julian) That's beautiful.

JULIAN

Thank you.

> *Julian continues to play.*

TILLY

What's your name?

JULIAN

Julian.

FRANK

Hello.

JOAN

Hello!

FRANCES

Hello!

LORENZO

Hello!

Julian stops playing.

JULIAN

Hello.

LORENZO

Excuse me, but would you mind telling us—are we almonds?
Do we look like almonds? Are we in Illinois?

JULIAN

I don't know.

TILLY

Julian—can you play something happy?

JULIAN

I think so.
It's difficult on a cello.

Julian begins to play a waltz.
Frances catches hold of Joan.

FRANCES

Joan. I can smell your hair.

JOAN

Oh, Frances!

LORENZO

Can almonds smell? Am I an almond?

TILLY

Lorenzo! For the last time. We don't care if we're almonds. The important thing is that we're together.

A waltz comes up as if on a victrola.
Julian plays along.

Frank—I adore you.

Tilly catches hold of Frank.

FRANK

Oh, Tilly.

FRANCES

Oh, Frank.

JOAN

Oh, Frances.

FRANCES

Oh, Joan.

LORENZO

Oh, Julian.

Julian puts down his cello.
Lorenzo catches hold of Julian.
They are happy.
They all dance a waltz.
The chandeliers glimmer.
The lights fade out.

THE END

Eurydice

This play is for my father

PRODUCTION HISTORY

Eurydice received its first workshop production in January 2001, in Providence, RI, at Brown University's New Play Festival (Mac Wellman, producer).

Eurydice received a workshop production at The Children's Theatre Company (Peter C. Brosius, Artistic Director; Teresa Eyring, Managing Director) in Minneapolis in September 2001. It was directed by Darron L. West and Rebecca Brown.

Eurydice received its world premiere at Madison Repertory Theatre (Richard Corley, Artistic Director; Tony Forman, Managing Director) in September 2003. The production was directed by Richard Corley; the set design was by Narelle Sissons, the lighting design was by Rand Ryan, the costume design was by Murell Horton, the sound design was by Darron L. West and movement was by Karen Hoyer; the stage manager was Lynn "Cubby" Terry, Jr. The cast was as follows:

EURYDICE	Laura Heisler
HER FATHER	John Lenertz
ORPHEUS	David Andrew McMahon
A NASTY INTERESTING MAN /	
THE LORD OF THE UNDERWORLD	Scot Morton
GRANDMOTHER / OLD WOMAN	Diane Dorsey
A CHORUS OF STONES:	
BIG STONE	Jody Reiss
LITTLE STONE	Polly Noonan
LOUD STONE	Karlie Nurse

Eurydice was produced at Berkeley Repertory Theatre (Tony Taccone, Artistic Director; Susan Medak, Managing Director) on October 15, 2004. The production was directed by Les Waters; the set design was by Scott Bradley, the lighting design was by Russell H. Champa, the costume design was by Meg Neville, the sound design was by Bray Poor; the stage manager was Michael Suenkel. The cast was as follows:

EURYDICE	Maria Dizzia
HER FATHER	Charles Shaw Robinson
ORPHEUS	Daniel Talbott
A NASTY INTERESTING MAN/	
THE LORD OF THE UNDERWORLD	Mark Zeisler
A CHORUS OF STONES:	
BIG STONE	Ramiz Monsef
LITTLE STONE	T. Edward Webster
LOUD STONE	Aimée Guillot

Characters

EURYDICE

HER FATHER

ORPHEUS

A NASTY INTERESTING MAN/
   THE LORD OF THE UNDERWORLD

A CHORUS OF STONES:
   BIG STONE
   LITTLE STONE
   LOUD STONE

Set

The set contains a raining elevator,
a water pump,
some rusty exposed pipes,
an abstracted River of Forgetfulness,
an old-fashioned glow-in-the-dark globe.

Notes

Eurydice and Orpheus should be played as though they are a little too young and a little too in love. They should resist the temptation to be "classical."

The underworld should resemble the world of *Alice in Wonderland* more than it resembles Hades.

The Stones might be played as though they are nasty children at a birthday party.

When people compose letters in this play they needn't actually scribble them—they can speak directly to the audience.

The set should allow for fluid transitions from moment to moment—from underworld to overworld and back again.

The play should be performed without an intermission.

First Movement

Scene 1

A young man—Orpheus—and a young woman—Eurydice.
They wear swimming outfits from the 1950s.
Orpheus makes a sweeping gesture with his arm, indicating the sky.

EURYDICE

All those birds? Thank you.

He nods. They make a quarter turn and he makes a sweeping gesture, indicating an invisible sea.

And—the sea! For me? When?

Orpheus opens his hands.

Now? It's mine already?

Orpheus nods.

Wow.

They kiss. He indicates the sky.

Surely not—surely not the sky and the stars too?!

Orpheus nods.

That's very generous.

Orpheus nods.

Perhaps too generous?

Orpheus shakes his head no.

Thank you.
Now—walk over there.

Orpheus walks in a straight line on an unseen boardwalk.

Don't look at me.

He turns his face away from hers and walks.

Now—stop.

He stops.
She runs and jumps into his arms.
He doesn't quite catch her and they fall down together.
She crawls on top of him and kisses his eyes.

What are you thinking about?

ORPHEUS

Music.

EURYDICE

How can you think about music? You either hear it or you don't.

ORPHEUS

I'm hearing it then.

EURYDICE

Oh.

Pause.

I read a book today.

ORPHEUS

Did you?

EURYDICE

Yes. It was very interesting.

ORPHEUS

That's good.

EURYDICE

Don't you want to know what it was about?

ORPHEUS

Of course.

EURYDICE

There were—stories—about people's lives—how some come out well—and others come out badly.

ORPHEUS

Do you love the book?

EURYDICE

Yes—I think so.

ORPHEUS

Why?

EURYDICE

It can be interesting to see if other people—like dead people who wrote books—agree or disagree with what you think.

ORPHEUS

Why?

EURYDICE

Because it makes you—a larger part of the human community. It had very interesting arguments.

ORPHEUS

Oh. And arguments that are interesting are good arguments?

EURYDICE

Well—yes.

ORPHEUS

I didn't know an argument should be interesting. I thought it should be right or wrong.

EURYDICE

Well, these particular arguments were very interesting.

ORPHEUS

Maybe you should make up your own thoughts. Instead of reading them in a book.

EURYDICE

I do. I do think up my own thoughts.

ORPHEUS

I know you do. I love how you love books. Don't be mad.

Pause.

I made up a song for you today.

EURYDICE

Did you?!

ORPHEUS

Yup. It's not *interesting* or *not interesting*. It just—is.

EURYDICE

Will you sing it for me?

ORPHEUS

It has too many parts.

EURYDICE

Let's go in the water.

They start walking, arm in arm,
on extensive unseen boardwalks, toward the water.

ORPHEUS

Wait—remember this melody.

He hums a bar of melody.

EURYDICE

I'm bad at remembering melodies. Why don't you remember it?

ORPHEUS

I have eleven other ones in my head, making for a total of twelve.
You have it?

EURYDICE

Yes. I think so.

ORPHEUS

Let's hear it.

She sings the melody.
She misses a few notes.
She's not the best singer in the world.

Pretty good. The rhythm's a little off. Here—clap it out.

She claps.
He claps the rhythmic sequence for her.
She tries to imitate.
She is still off.

ORPHEUS

EURYDICE

Is that right?

ORPHEUS

We'll practice.

EURYDICE

I don't need to know about rhythm. I have my books.

ORPHEUS

Don't books have rhythm?

EURYDICE

Kind of. Let's go in the water.

ORPHEUS

Will you remember my melody under the water?

EURYDICE

Yes! I WILL ALWAYS REMEMBER YOUR MELODY! It will be imprinted on my heart like wax.

ORPHEUS

Thank you.

EURYDICE

You're welcome. When are you going to play me the whole song?

ORPHEUS

When I get twelve instruments.

EURYDICE

Where are you going to get twelve instruments?

ORPHEUS

I'm going to make each strand of your hair into an instrument. Your hair will stand on end as it plays my music and become a hair orchestra. It will fly you up into the sky.

EURYDICE

I don't know if I want to be an instrument.

ORPHEUS

Why?

EURYDICE

Won't I fall down when the song ends?

ORPHEUS

That's true. But the clouds will be so moved by your music that they will fill up with water until they become heavy and you'll sit on one and fall gently down to earth. How about that?

EURYDICE

Okay.

> *They stop walking for a moment.*
> *They gaze at each other.*

ORPHEUS

It's settled then.

EURYDICE

What is?

ORPHEUS

Your hair will be my orchestra and—I love you.

> *Pause.*

ORPHEUS

EURYDICE

I love you, too.

ORPHEUS

How will you remember?

EURYDICE

That I love you?

ORPHEUS

Yes.

EURYDICE

That's easy. I can't help it.

ORPHEUS

You never know. I'd better tie a string around your finger to remind you.

EURYDICE

Is there string at the ocean?

ORPHEUS

I always have string. In case I come upon a broken instrument.

He takes out a string from his pocket.
He takes her left hand.

This hand.

He wraps string deliberately around her fourth finger.

Is this too tight?

EURYDICE

No—it's fine.

ORPHEUS

There—now you'll remember.

EURYDICE

That's a very particular finger.

ORPHEUS

Yes.

EURYDICE

You're aware of that?

ORPHEUS

Yes.

EURYDICE

How aware?

ORPHEUS

Very aware.

EURYDICE

Orpheus—are we?

ORPHEUS

You tell me.

EURYDICE

Yes.
I think so.

ORPHEUS

You *think* so?

EURYDICE

I wasn't thinking.
I mean—yes. Just: Yes.

ORPHEUS

Yes?

EURYDICE

Yes.

ORPHEUS

Yes!

EURYDICE

Yes!

ORPHEUS

May our lives be full of music!

Music.
He picks her up and throws her into the sky.

EURYDICE

Maybe you could also get me another ring—a gold one—to put over the string one. You know?

ORPHEUS

Whatever makes you happy. Do you still have my melody?

EURYDICE

It's right here.

She points to her temple.
They look at each other. A silence.

What are you thinking about?

ORPHEUS

Music.

Her face falls.

Just kidding. I was thinking about you. And music.

EURYDICE

Let's go in the water. I'll race you!

She puts on her swimming goggles.

ORPHEUS

I'll race *you*!

EURYDICE

I'll race *you*!

ORPHEUS

I'll race *you*!

EURYDICE

I'll race *you*!

They race toward the water.

Scene 2

The Father, dressed in a gray suit, reads from a letter.

FATHER

Dear Eurydice,

A letter for you on your wedding day.

There is no choice of any importance in life but the choosing of a beloved. I haven't met Orpheus, but he seems like a serious young man. I understand he's a musician.

If I were to give a speech at your wedding I would start with one or two funny jokes, and then I might offer some words of advice. I would say:

> Cultivate the arts of dancing and small talk.
> Everything in moderation.
> Court the companionship and respect of dogs.
> Grilling a fish or toasting bread without burning requires singleness of purpose, vigilance and steadfast watching.
> Keep quiet about politics, but vote for the right man.
> Take care to change the light bulbs.

Continue to give yourself to others because that's the ultimate satisfaction in life—to love, accept, honor and help others.

As for me, this is what it's like being dead:
the atmosphere smells. And there are strange high-pitched noises—like a tea kettle always boiling over. But it doesn't seem to bother anyone. And, for the most part, there is a pleasant atmosphere and you can work and socialize, much like at home. I'm working in the business world and it seems that, here, you can better see the far-reaching consequences of your actions.

Also, I am one of the few dead people who still remembers how to read and write. That's a secret. If anyone finds out, they might dip me in the River again.

I write you letters. I don't know how to get them to you.

Love,
Your Father

He drops the letter as though into a mail slot.
It falls on the ground.
Wedding music.
In the underworld, the Father walks in a
straight line as though he is walking his daughter down the aisle.
He is affectionate, then solemn, then glad, then solemn, then amused,
then solemn.
He looks at his imaginary daughter; he looks straight ahead; he
acknowledges the guests at the wedding; he gets choked-up; he looks at
his daughter and smiles an embarrassed smile for getting choked-up.
He looks straight ahead, calm.
He walks.
Suddenly, he checks his watch. He exits, in a hurry.

Scene 3

Eurydice, by a water pump.
The noise of a party, from far off.

EURYDICE

I hate parties.

And a wedding party is the biggest party of all.

All the guests arrived and Orpheus is taking a shower.

He's always taking a shower when the guests arrive so he doesn't have to greet them.

Then I have to greet them.

A wedding is for daughters and fathers. The mothers all dress up, trying to look like young women. But a wedding is for a father and a daughter. They stop being married to each other on that day.

I always thought there would be more interesting people at my wedding.

She drinks a cup of water from the water pump.
A Nasty Interesting Man, wearing a trench coat, appears.

MAN

Are you a homeless person?

EURYDICE

No.

MAN

Oh. I'm on my way to a party where there are really very interesting people. Would you like to join me?

EURYDICE

No. I just left my own party.

MAN

You were giving a party and you just—left?

EURYDICE

I was thirsty.

MAN

You must be a very interesting person, to leave your own party like that.

EURYDICE

Thank you.

MAN

You mustn't care at all what other people think of you. I always say that's a mark of a really interesting person, don't you?

EURYDICE

I guess.

MAN

So would you like to accompany me to this interesting affair?

EURYDICE

No, thank you. I just got married, you see.

MAN

Oh—lots of people do that.

EURYDICE

That's true—lots of people do.

MAN

What's your name?

EURYDICE

Eurydice.

He looks at her, hungry.

MAN

Eurydice.

EURYDICE

Good-bye, then.

MAN

Good-bye.

She exits. He sits by the water pump.
He notices a letter on the ground.
He picks it up and reads it.
To himself:

Dear Eurydice . . .

Musty dripping sounds.

Scene 4

The Father tries to remember how to do the jitterbug in the underworld.
He does the jitterbug with an imaginary partner.
He has fun.

Orpheus and Eurydice dance together at their wedding.
They are happy.
They have had some champagne.
They sing together:

ORPHEUS AND EURYDICE

Don't sit under the apple tree
With anyone else but me
Anyone else but me
Anyone else but me
No no no.
Don't sit under the apple tree
With anyone else but me
Till I come marching home . . .

On the other side of the stage,
the Father checks his watch.
He stops doing the jitterbug.
He exits, in a hurry.

Don't go walking down lover's lane
With anyone else but me

Anyone else but me
Anyone else but me
No no no.
Don't go walking down lover's lane
With anyone else but me
Till I come marching home . . .

EURYDICE

I'm warm. Are you warm?

ORPHEUS

Yes!

EURYDICE

I'm going to get a drink of water.

ORPHEUS

Don't go.

EURYDICE

I'll be right back.

ORPHEUS

Promise?

EURYDICE

Yes.

ORPHEUS

I can't stand to let you out of my sight today.

EURYDICE

Silly goose.

They kiss.

Scene 5

Eurydice at the water pump,
getting a glass of water.
The Nasty Interesting Man appears.

EURYDICE

Oh—you're still here.

MAN

Yes. I forgot to tell you something. I have a letter. Addressed to
Eurydice—that's you—from your father.

EURYDICE

That's not possible.

MAN

He wrote down some thoughts—for your wedding day.

EURYDICE

Let me see.

MAN

I left it at home. It got delivered to my elegant high-rise apartment
by mistake.

EURYDICE

Why didn't you say so before?

MAN

You left in such a hurry.

EURYDICE

From my father?

MAN

Yes.

EURYDICE

You're sure?

MAN

Yes.

EURYDICE

I knew he'd send something!

MAN

It'll just take a moment. I live around the block. What an interesting dress you're wearing.

EURYDICE

Thank you.

Scene 6

Orpheus, from the water pump.

ORPHEUS

Eurydice?
Eurydice!

Scene 7

The sound of a door closing.
The Interesting Apartment—a giant loft space with no furniture.
Eurydice and the Man enter, panting.

MAN

Voilà.

EURYDICE

You're very high up.

MAN

Yes. I am.

EURYDICE

I feel a little faint.

MAN

It'll pass.

EURYDICE

Have you ever thought about installing an elevator?

MAN

No. I prefer stairs.
I think architecture is so interesting, don't you?

EURYDICE

Oh, yes. So, where's the letter?

MAN

But isn't this an interesting building?

EURYDICE

It's so—high up.

MAN

Yes.

EURYDICE

There's no one here. I thought you were having a party.

MAN

I like to celebrate things quietly. With a few other interesting people. Don't you?

She tilts her head to the side and stares at him.

Would you like some champagne?

EURYDICE

Maybe some water.

MAN

Water it is! Make yourself comfortable.

He switches on Brazilian mood music. He exits.
Eurydice looks around.

EURYDICE

I can't stay long!

She looks out the window. She is very high up.

I can see my wedding from here!
The people are so small—they're dancing!
There's Orpheus!
He's not dancing.

MAN

(Shouting from offstage) So, who's this guy you're marrying?

EURYDICE

(Shouting) His name is Orpheus.

As he attempts to open champagne offstage:

MAN

Orpheus. Not a very interesting name. I've heard it before.

EURYDICE

Maybe you've heard of him. He's kind of famous. He plays the
most beautiful music in the world, actually.

MAN

I can't hear you!

EURYDICE

So the letter was delivered—here—today?

MAN

That's right.

EURYDICE

Through the post?

MAN

It was—mysterious.

The sound of champagne popping.
He enters with one glass of champagne.

Voilà.

He drinks the champagne.

So. Eurydice. Tell me one thing. Name me one person you find interesting.

EURYDICE

Why?

MAN

Just making conversation.

He sways a little to the music.

EURYDICE

Right. Um—all the interesting people I know are dead or speak French.

MAN

Well, I don't speak French, Eurydice.

He takes one step toward her.
She takes one step back.

EURYDICE

I'm sorry. I have to go. There's no letter, is there?

MAN

Of course there's a letter. It's right here. *(He pats his breast pocket)*
Eurydice. I'm not interesting, but I'm strong. You could teach me
to be interesting. I would listen. Orpheus is too busy listening to
his own thoughts. There's music in his head. Try to pluck the music
out and it bites you. I'll bet you had an interesting thought today,
for instance.

She tilts her head to the side, quizzical.

I bet you're always having them, the way you tilt your head to the
side and stare . . .

She jerks her head back up.
Musty dripping sounds.

EURYDICE

I feel dizzy all of a sudden. I want my husband. I think I'd better
go now.

MAN

You're free to go, whenever you like.

EURYDICE

I know.
I think I'll go now, in fact.
I'll just take my letter first, if you don't mind.

She holds out her hand for the letter.
He takes her hand.

MAN

Relax.

She takes her hand away.

EURYDICE

Good-bye.

She turns to exit.
He blocks the doorway.

MAN

Wait. Eurydice. Don't go. I love you.

EURYDICE

Oh no.

MAN

You need to get yourself a real man. A man with broad shoulders
like me. Orpheus has long fingers that would tremble to pet a bull
or pluck a bee from a hive—

EURYDICE

How do you know about my husband's fingers?

MAN

A man who can put his big arm around your little shoulders as he
leads you through the crowd, a man who answers the door at parties . . . A man with big hands, with big stupid hands like potatoes,
a man who can carry a cow in labor.

The Man backs Eurydice against the wall.

My lips were meant to kiss your eyelids, that's obvious!

EURYDICE

Close your eyes, then!

He closes his eyes, expecting a kiss.
She takes the letter from his breast pocket.

She slips by him and opens the door to the stairwell.
He opens his eyes.
She looks at the letter.

It's his handwriting!

MAN

Of course it is!

He reaches for her.

EURYDICE

Good-bye.

She runs for the stairs.
She wavers, off-balance, at the top of the stairwell.

MAN

Don't do that, you'll trip! There are six hundred stairs!

EURYDICE

Orpheus!

From the water pump:

ORPHEUS

Eurydice!

She runs, trips and pitches down the stairs, holding her letter.
She follows the letter down, down down . . .
Blackout.
A clatter. Strange sounds—xylophones, brass bands, sounds of falling,
sounds of vertigo.
Sounds of breathing.

SARAH RUHL

356

SARAH RUHL

She slips by him and opens the door to the stairwell.
He opens his eyes.
She looks at the letter.

It's his handwriting!

MAN

Of course it is!

He reaches for her.

EURYDICE

Good-bye.

She runs for the stairs.
She wavers, off-balance, at the top of the stairwell.

MAN

Don't do that, you'll trip! There are six hundred stairs!

EURYDICE

Orpheus!

From the water pump:

ORPHEUS

Eurydice!

She runs, trips and pitches down the stairs, holding her letter.
She follows the letter down, down down . . .
Blackout.
A clatter. Strange sounds—xylophones, brass bands, sounds of falling, sounds of vertigo.
Sounds of breathing.

356

SECOND MOVEMENT

The underworld.
There is no set change.
Strange watery noises.
Drip, drip, drip.
The movement to the underworld is marked
by the entrance of stones.

Scene 1

THE STONES

We are a chorus of stones.

LITTLE STONE

I'm a little stone.

BIG STONE

I'm a big stone.

LOUD STONE

I'm a loud stone.

SARAH RUHL

THE STONES

We are all three stones.

LITTLE STONE

We live with the dead people in the land of the dead.

BIG STONE

Eurydice was a great musician. Orpheus was his wife.

LOUD STONE

(Correcting Big Stone) Orpheus was a great musician. Eurydice was his wife. She died.

LITTLE STONE

Then he played the saddest music.
Even we—

THE STONES

the stones—

LITTLE STONE

cried when we heard it.

The sound of three drops of water hitting a pond.

Oh, look,
she is coming into the land of the dead now.

BIG STONE

Oh!

LOUD STONE

Oh!

LITTLE STONE

Oh!
We might say: "Poor Eurydice"—

EURYDICE

but stones don't feel bad for
dead people.

> *The sound of an elevator ding.*
> *An elevator door opens.*
> *Inside the elevator, it is raining.*
> *Eurydice gets rained on inside the elevator.*
> *She carries a suitcase and an umbrella.*
> *She is dressed in the kind of 1930s suit*
> *that women wore when they eloped.*
> *She looks bewildered.*
> *The sound of an elevator ding.*
> *Eurydice steps out of the elevator.*
> *The elevator door closes.*
> *She walks toward the audience and opens her mouth,*
> *trying to speak.*
> *There is a great humming noise.*
> *She closes her mouth.*
> *The humming noise stops.*
> *She opens her mouth for the second time,*
> *attempting to tell her story to the audience.*
> *There is a great humming noise.*
> *She closes her mouth—the humming noise stops.*
> *She has a tantrum of despair.*
> *The Stones, to the audience:*

THE STONES

Eurydice wants to speak to you.
But she can't speak your language anymore.
She talks in the language of dead people now.

LITTLE STONE

It's a very quiet language.

LOUD STONE

Like if the pores in your face
opened up and talked.

BIG STONE

Like potatoes sleeping in the dirt.

*Little Stone and Loud Stone look at Big Stone as though that were a
dumb thing to say.*

LITTLE STONE

Pretend that you understand her
or she'll be embarrassed.

BIG STONE

Yes—pretend for a moment
that you understand
the language of stones.

LOUD STONE

Listen to her the way you would listen
to your own daughter
if she died too young
and tried to speak to you
across long distances.

*Eurydice shakes out her umbrella.
She approaches the audience.
This time, she can speak.*

EURYDICE

There was a roar, and a coldness—
I think my husband was with me.
What was my husband's name?

Eurydice turns to the Stones.

My husband's name? Do you know it?

The Stones shrug their shoulders.

How strange. I don't remember.
It was horrible to see his face

when I died. His eyes were
two black birds
and they flew to me.
I said: no—stay where you are—
he needs you in order to see!
When I got through the cold
they made me swim in a river
and I forgot his name.
I forgot all the names.
I know his name starts with my mouth
shaped like a ball of twine—
Oar—oar.
I forget.
They took me to a tiny boat.
I only just fit inside.
I looked at the oars
and I wanted to cry.
I tried to cry but I just drooled a little.
I'll try now.

    She tries to cry but finds that she can't.

What happiness it would be to cry.

    She takes a breath.

I was not lonely
only alone with myself
begging myself not to leave my own body
but I *was* leaving.
Good-bye, head—I said—
it inclined itself a little, as though to nod to me
in a solemn kind of way.

    She turns to the Stones.

How do you say good-bye to yourself?

They shake their heads.
A train whistle.
Eurydice steps onto a platform, surveying a large crowd.

A train!

LITTLE STONE

The station is like a train but
there is no train.

BIG STONE

The train has wheels that are not wheels.

LOUD STONE

There is the opposite of a wheel and the
opposite of smoke and the opposite of a train.

A train pulls away.

EURYDICE

Oh! I'm waiting for someone to meet me, I think.

Eurydice's Father approaches and takes her baggage.

FATHER

Eurydice.

EURYDICE

(To the Stones) At last, a porter to meet me!
(To the Father) Do you happen to know where the bank is? I need
money. I've just arrived. I need to exchange my money at the
Bureau de Change. I didn't bring traveler's checks because I left
in such a hurry. They didn't even let me pack my suitcase. There's
nothing in it! That's funny, right? Funny—ha ha! I suppose I can
buy new clothes here. I would *really* love a bath.

FATHER

Eurydice!

EURYDICE

What is that language you're speaking? It gives me tingles. Say it again.

FATHER

Eurydice!

EURYDICE

Oooh—it's like a fruit! Again!

FATHER

Eurydice—I'm your father.

EURYDICE

(Strangely imitating) Eurydice—I'm your father! How funny! You remind me of something but I can't understand a word you're saying. Say it again!

FATHER

Your father.

THE STONES

(To the Father) Shut up, shut up!
She doesn't understand you.
She's dead now, too.
You have to speak in the language of stones.

FATHER

(To Eurydice) You're dead now. I'm dead, too.

EURYDICE

Yes, that's right. I need a reservation. For the fancy hotel.

FATHER

When you were alive, I was your father.

THE STONES

Father is not a word that dead people understand.

BIG STONE

He is what we call subversive.

FATHER

When you were alive, I was your tree.

EURYDICE

My tree! Yes, the tall one in the backyard! I used to sit all day in its shade!

She sits at the feet of her father.

Ah—there—shade!

LITTLE STONE

There is a problem here.

EURYDICE

Is there any entertainment at the hotel? Any dancing ladies? Like with the great big fans?

FATHER

I named you Eurydice. Your mother named all the other children. But Eurydice I chose for you.

BIG STONE

Be careful, sir.

FATHER

Eurydice. I wanted to remember your name. I asked the Stones. They said: forget the names—the names make you remember.

LOUD STONE

We told you how it works!

FATHER

One day it would not stop raining.

I heard your name inside the rain—somewhere between the drops—I saw falling letters. Each letter of your name—I began to translate.

E—I remembered elephants. U—I remembered ulcers and under. R—I remembered reindeers. I saw them putting their black noses into snow. Y—youth and yellow. D—dog, dig, daughter, day. Time poured into my head. The days of the week. Hours, months . . .

EURYDICE

The tree talks so beautifully.

THE STONES

Don't listen!

EURYDICE

I feel suddenly hungry! Where is the porter who met me at the station?

FATHER

Here I am.

EURYDICE

I would like a continental breakfast, please. Maybe some rolls and butter. Oh—and jam. Please take my suitcase to my room, if you would.

FATHER

I'm sorry, miss, but there are no rooms here.

EURYDICE

What? No rooms? Where do people sleep?

FATHER

People don't sleep here.

EURYDICE

I have to say I'm very disappointed. It's been such a tiring day. I've been traveling all day—first on a river, then on an elevator that rained, then on a train . . . I thought someone would meet me at the station . . .

Eurydice is on the verge of tears.

THE STONES

Don't cry! Don't cry!

EURYDICE

I don't know where I am and there are all these stones and I hate them! They're horrible! I want a bath! I thought someone would meet me at the station!

FATHER

Don't be sad. I'll take your luggage to your room.

THE STONES

THERE ARE NO ROOMS!

He picks up her luggage.
He gives the Stones a dirty look.
The sound of water in rusty pipes.

Scene 2

Orpheus writes a letter to Eurydice.

ORPHEUS

Dear Eurydice,

I miss you.

No—that's not enough.

He crumples up the letter.
He writes a new letter.
He thinks.
He writes:

Dear Eurydice,

Symphony for twelve instruments.

A pause.
He hears the music in his head.
He conducts.

Love,
Orpheus

He drops the letter as though into a mail slot.

Scene 3

The Father creates a room out of string for Eurydice.
He makes four walls and a door out of string.
Time passes.
It takes time to build a room out of string.
Eurydice observes the underworld.
There isn't much to observe.
She plays hop-scotch without chalk.
Every so often,
the Father looks at her,
happy to see her,
while he makes her room out of string.
She looks back at him, polite.

Scene 4

The Father has completed the string room.
He gestures for Eurydice to enter.
She enters with her suitcase.

EURYDICE

Thank you. That will do.

She nods to her Father.
He doesn't leave.

Oh.
I suppose you want a tip.

He shakes his head no.

Would you run a bath for me?

FATHER

Yes, miss.

He exits the string room.
Eurydice opens her suitcase.
She is surprised to find nothing inside.
She sits down inside her suitcase.

Scene 5

ORPHEUS

Dear Eurydice,

I love you. I'm going to find you. I play the saddest music now that you're gone. You know I hate writing letters. I'll give this letter to a worm. I hope he finds you.

Love,
Orpheus

He drops the letter as though into a mail slot.

Scene 6

The Father enters the string room with a letter on a silver tray.

FATHER

There is a letter for you, miss.

EURYDICE

A letter?

He nods.

A letter.

He hands her the letter.

It's addressed to you.

EURYDICE

There's dirt on it.

> *Eurydice wipes the dirt off the letter.*
> *She opens it.*
> *She scrutinizes it.*
> *She does not know how to read it.*
> *She puts it on the ground, takes off her shoes,*
> *stands on the letter, and shuts her eyes.*
> *She thinks, without language for the thought,*
> *the melody: There's no place like home . . .*

FATHER

Miss.

EURYDICE

What is it?

FATHER

Would you like me to *read* you the letter?

EURYDICE

Read me the letter?

FATHER

You can't do it with your feet.

The Father guides her off the letter, picks it up and begins to read.

It's addressed to Eurydice. That's you.

EURYDICE

That's you.

FATHER

You.
It says: I love you.

EURYDICE

I love you?

FATHER

It's like your tree.

EURYDICE

Tall?

The Father considers.

Green?

FATHER

It's like sitting in the shade.

EURYDICE

Oh.

FATHER

It's like sitting in the shade with no clothes on.

EURYDICE

Oh!—yes.

FATHER

(Reading) I'm going to find you. I play the saddest music—

EURYDICE

Music?

He whistles a note.

FATHER

It's like that.

She smiles.

EURYDICE

Go on.

FATHER

You know I hate writing letters. I'll give this letter to a worm. I hope he finds you.

Love,
Orpheus

EURYDICE

Orpheus?

FATHER

Orpheus.

A pause.

EURYDICE

That word!
It's like—I can't breathe.
Orpheus! My husband.

Scene 7

ORPHEUS

Dear Eurydice,

Last night I dreamed that we climbed Mount Olympus and we started to make love and all the strands of your hair were

little faucets and water was streaming out of your head and
I said, why is water coming out of your hair? And you said,
gravity is very compelling.

And then we jumped off Mount Olympus and flew through
the clouds and you held your knee to your chest because you
skinned it on a sharp cloud and then we fell into a salty lake.
Then I woke up and the window frightened me and I thought:
Eurydice is dead. Then I thought—who is Eurydice? Then
the whole room started to float and I thought: what are people? Then my bed clothes smiled at me with a crooked green
mouth and I thought: who am I? It scares me, Eurydice.

Please come back.

Love,
Orpheus

Scene 8

Eurydice and her father in the string room.

FATHER

Did you get my letters?

EURYDICE

No! You wrote me letters?

FATHER

Every day.

EURYDICE

What did they say?

FATHER

Oh—nothing much. The usual stuff.

EURYDICE

Tell me the names of my mother and brothers and sisters.

FATHER

I don't think that's a good idea. It will make you sad.

EURYDICE

I want to know.

FATHER

It's a long time to be sad.

EURYDICE

I'd rather be sad.

THE STONES

Being sad is not allowed! Act like a stone.

Scene 9

Time shifts.
Eurydice and her father in the string room.

EURYDICE

Teach me another.

FATHER

Ostracize.

EURYDICE

What does it mean?

FATHER

To exclude. The Greeks decided who to banish. They wrote the name of the banished person on a white piece of pottery called ostrakon.

EURYDICE

Ostrakon.
Another.

FATHER

Peripatetic. From the Greek. It means to walk slowly, speaking of weighty matters, in bare feet.

EURYDICE

Peripatetic: a learned fruit, wandering through the snow. Another.

FATHER

Defunct.

EURYDICE

Defunct.

FATHER

It means dead in a very abrupt way. Not the way I died, which was slowly. But all at once, in cowboy boots.

EURYDICE

Tell me a story of when you were little.

FATHER

Well, there was the time your uncle shot at me with a BB gun and I was mad at him so I swallowed a nail.

Then there was the time I went to a dude ranch and I was riding a horse and I lassoed a car. The lady driving the car got out and spanked me. And your grandmother spanked me, too.

EURYDICE

Remember the Christmas when she gave me a doll and I said, "If I see one more doll I'm going to throw up"?

FATHER

I think Grammy was a little surprised when you said that.

EURYDICE

Tell me a story about your mother.

FATHER

The most vivid recollection I have of Mother was seeing her at parties and in the house playing piano. When she was younger she was extremely animated. She could really play the piano. She could play everything by ear. They called her Flaming Sally.

EURYDICE

I never saw Grammy play the piano.

FATHER

She was never the same after my father died. My father was a very gentle man.

EURYDICE

Tell me a story about your father.

FATHER

My father and I used to duck hunt. He would call up old Frank the night before and ask, "Where are the ducks moving tonight?" Frank was a guide and a farmer. Old Frank, he could really call the ducks. It was hard for me to kill the poor little ducks, but you get caught up in the fervor of it. You'd get as many as ten ducks.

If you went over the limit—there were only so many ducks per person—Father would throw the ducks to the side of the creek we were paddling on and make sure there was no game warden. If the warden was gone, he'd run back and get the extra ducks and throw them in the back of the car. My father was never a great conversationalist, but he loved to rhapsodize about hunting. He would always say, if I ever have to die, it's in a duck pond. And he did.

EURYDICE

There was something I always wanted to ask you. It was—how to do something—or—a story—or someone's name—I forget.

FATHER

Don't worry. You'll remember. There's plenty of time.

Scene 10

Orpheus writes a letter.

ORPHEUS

Dear Eurydice,

I wonder if you miss reading books in the underworld.

Orpheus holds the Collected Works of Shakespeare
with a long string attached.
He drops it slowly to the ground.

Scene 11

Eurydice holds the Collected Works of Shakespeare.

EURYDICE

What is this?

She opens it. She doesn't understand it.
She throws the book on the ground.

What are you?

She is wary of it, as though it might bite her.
She tries to understand the book.
She tries to make the book do something.
To the book:

What do you do?
What do you DO?!
Are you a thing or a person?
Say something!
I hate you!

She stands on the book, trying to read it.

Damn you!

She throws the book at the Stones.
They duck.

That is not allowed!

Drops of water.
Time passes.
The Father picks up the book.
He brushes it off.
The Father teaches Eurydice how to read.
She looks over his shoulder as he reads out loud from King Lear.

FATHER

We two alone will sing like birds in the cage.
When thou dost ask my blessing, I'll kneel down
And ask of thee forgiveness; so we'll live,
And pray and sing . . .

Scene 12

Orpheus, with a telephone.

ORPHEUS

For Eurydice—E, U, R, Y—that's right. No, there's no last name.
It's not like that. What? No, I don't know the country. I don't
know the city either. I don't know the street. I don't know—it
probably starts with a vowel. Could you just—would you mind
checking please—I would really appreciate it. You can't enter a
name without a city? Why not? Well, thank you for trying. Wait—
miss—it's a special case. She's dead. Well, thank you for trying.
You have a nice day, too.

He hangs up.

I'll find you. Don't move!

He fingers a glow-in-the-dark globe, looking for Eurydice.

Scene 13

Eurydice and her father in the string room.

EURYDICE

Tell me another story of when you were little.

FATHER

Let's see.
There was my first piano recital. I was playing "I Got Rhythm."
I played the first few chords and I couldn't remember the rest.
I ran out of the room and locked myself in the bathroom.

EURYDICE

Then what happened?

FATHER

Your grandmother pulled me out of the bathroom and made me apologize to everyone in the auditorium. I never played piano after that. But I still know the first four chords—let's see—

He plays the chords in the air with his hands.

Da Da *Dee* Da
Da Da *Dee* Da
Da Da *Dee* Da . . .

EURYDICE

What are the words?

FATHER

I can't remember.
Let's see . . .

Da Da *Dee* Da
Da Da *Dee* da . . .

They both start singing to the tune of "I Got Rhythm":

FATHER AND EURYDICE

Da da *Dee* Da
Da da *Dee* Da
Da da *Dee* Da
Da dee da da doo dee dee da.

Da da Da da
Da da Da da
Da Da da Da
Da da da . . .

Da da *Dee* Da
Da da *dee* da . . .

THE STONES

WHAT IS THAT NOISE?

LITTLE STONE

Stop singing!

LOUD STONE

STOP SINGING!

BIG STONE

Neither of you can carry a tune.

LITTLE STONE

It's awful.

THE STONES

DEAD PEOPLE CAN'T SING!

EURYDICE

I'm not a very good singer.

FATHER

Neither am I.

THE STONES

(To the Father) Stop singing and go to work!

Scene 14

The Father leaves for work.
He takes his briefcase.
He waves to Eurydice.
She waves back.
She is alone in the string room.
She touches the string.
A child, the Lord of the Underworld, enters on his red tricycle.
Music from a heavy metal band accompanies his entrance.
His clothes and his hat are too small for him.
He stops pedaling at the entrance to the string room.

CHILD

Knock, knock.

EURYDICE

Who's there?

CHILD

I am Lord of the Underworld.

EURYDICE

Very funny.

CHILD

I am.

EURYDICE

Prove it.

CHILD

I can do chin-ups inside your bones. Close your eyes.

She closes her eyes.

EURYDICE

Ow.

CHILD

See?

EURYDICE

What do you want?

CHILD

You're pretty.

EURYDICE

I'm dead.

CHILD

You're pretty.

EURYDICE

You're little.

CHILD

I grow downward. Like a turnip.

EURYDICE

What do you want?

CHILD

I wanted to see if you were comfortable.

EURYDICE

Comfortable?

CHILD

You're not itchy?

EURYDICE

No.

CHILD

That's good. Sometimes our residents get itchy. Then I scratch them.

EURYDICE

I'm not itchy.

CHILD

What's all this string?

EURYDICE

It's my room.

CHILD

Rooms are not allowed!
(To the Stones) Tell her.

THE STONES

Rooms are not allowed!

CHILD

Who made your room?

EURYDICE

My father.

CHILD

Fathers are not allowed! Where is he?

EURYDICE

He's at work.

CHILD

We'll have to dip you in the river again and make sure you're good and dunked.

EURYDICE

Please, don't.

CHILD

Oooh—say that again. It's nice.

EURYDICE

Please don't.

CHILD

Say it in my ear.

EURYDICE

(Toward his ear) Please, don't.

CHILD

I like that.
(A seduction) I'll huff and I'll puff and I'll blow your house down!

   He blows on her face.

I mean that in the nicest possible way.

EURYDICE

I have a husband.

CHILD

Husbands are for children. You need a lover. I'll be back.

   To the Stones:

See that she's . . . comfortable.

THE STONES

We will!

CHILD

Good-bye.

EURYDICE

Good-bye.

THE STONES

Good-bye.

CHILD

I'm growing. Can you tell? I'm growing!

He laughs his hysterical laugh and speeds away on his red tricycle.

Scene 15

A big storm. The sound of rain on a roof.
Orpheus in a rain slicker.
Shouting above the storm:

ORPHEUS

If a drop of water enters the soil
at a particular angle, with a particular pitch,
what's to say a man can't ride one note
into the earth like a fireman's pole?

He puts a bucket on the ground to catch rain falling.
He looks at the rain falling into the bucket.
He tunes his guitar, trying to make the pitch of each note
correspond with the pitch of each water drop.
Orpheus wonders if one particular pitch
might lead him to the underworld.
Orpheus wonders if the pitch
he is searching for might

correspond to the pitch of a drop
of rain, as it enters the soil.
A pitch.

Eurydice—did you hear that?

Another pitch.

Eurydice? That's the note. That one, right there.

Scene 16

Eurydice and her father in the string room.

EURYDICE

Orpheus never liked words. He had his music. He would get a funny look on his face and I would say what are you thinking about and he would always be thinking about music.

If we were in a restaurant, sometimes I would get embarrassed because Orpheus looked sullen and wouldn't talk to me and I thought people felt sorry for me. I should have realized that women envied me. Their husbands talked too much.

But I wanted to talk to him about my notions. I was working on a new philosophical system. It involved hats.

This is what it is to love an artist: The moon is always rising above your house. The houses of your neighbors look dull and lacking in moonlight. But he is always going away from you. Inside his head there is always something more beautiful.

Orpheus said the mind is a slide ruler. It can fit around anything. Words can mean anything. Show me your body, he said. It only means one thing.

She looks at her father, embarrassed for revealing too much.

Or maybe two or three things. But only one thing at a time.

Scene 17

ORPHEUS

Eurydice!

Before I go down there, I won't practice my music. Some say practice. But practice is a word invented by cowards. The animals don't have a word for practice. A gazelle does not run for practice. He runs because he is scared or he is hungry. A bird doesn't sing for practice. She sings because she's happy or sad. So I say: store it up. The music sounds better in my head than it does in the world. When songs are pressing against my throat, then, only then, I will go down and sing for the devils and they will cry through their parched throats.

Eurydice, don't kiss a dead man. Their lips look red and tempting but put your tongue in their mouths and it tastes like oatmeal. I know how much you hate oatmeal.

I'm going the way of death.

Here is my plan: tonight, when I go to bed, I will turn off the light and put a straw in my mouth. When I fall asleep, I will crawl through the straw and my breath will push me like a great wind into the darkness and I will sing your name and I will arrive. I have consulted the almanacs, the footstools, and the architects, and everyone agrees. Wait for me.

Love,
Orpheus

Scene 18

EURYDICE

I got a letter. From Orpheus.

FATHER

You sound serious. Nothing wrong I hope.

EURYDICE

No.

FATHER

What did he say?

EURYDICE

He says he's going to come find me.

FATHER

How?

EURYDICE

He's going to sing.

Scene 19

Darkness.
An unearthly light surrounds Orpheus.
He holds a straw up to his lips in slow motion.
He blows into the straw.
The sound of breath.
He disappears.

Scene 20

The sound of a knock.

LITTLE STONE

Someone is knocking!

BIG STONE

Who is it?

LOUD STONE

Who is it?

The sound of three loud knocks, insistent.

THE STONES

NO ONE KNOCKS AT THE DOOR OF THE DEAD!

THIRD MOVEMENT

Scene 1

Orpheus stands at the gates of hell.
He opens his mouth.
He looks like he's singing, but he's silent.
Music surrounds him.
The melody Orpheus hummed in the first scene,
repeated over and over again.
Raspberries, peaches and plums drop from the ceiling into the River.
Orpheus keeps singing.
The Stones weep.
They look at their tears, bewildered.
Orpheus keeps singing.
The child comes out of a trapdoor.

CHILD

Who are you?

ORPHEUS

I am Orpheus.

CHILD

I am Lord of the Underworld.

ORPHEUS

But you're so young!

CHILD

Don't be rude.

ORPHEUS

Sorry.
Did you like my music?

CHILD

No. I prefer happy music with a nice beat.

ORPHEUS

Oh.

CHILD

You've come for Eurydice.

ORPHEUS

Yes!

CHILD

And you thought singing would get you through the gates of hell.

ORPHEUS

See here. I want my wife.
What do I have to do?

CHILD

You'll have to do more than sing.

ORPHEUS

I'm not sure what you mean, sir.

CHILD

Start walking home. Your wife just might be on the road behind
you. We make it real nice here. So people want to stick around.
As you walk, keep your eyes facing front. If you look back at
her—poof! She's gone.

ORPHEUS

I can't look at her?

CHILD

No.

ORPHEUS

Why?

CHILD

Because.

ORPHEUS

Because?

CHILD

Because.
Do you understand me?

ORPHEUS

I look straight ahead. That's all?

CHILD

Yes.

ORPHEUS

That's easy.

CHILD

Good.

The child smiles. He exits.

Scene 2

Eurydice and her father.

EURYDICE

I hear him at the gates! That's his music!
He's come to save me!

FATHER

Do you want to go with him?

EURYDICE

Yes, of course!

Oh—you'll be lonely, won't you?

FATHER

No, no. You should go to your husband. You should have grand-
children. You'll all come down and meet me one day.

EURYDICE

Are you sure?

FATHER

You should love your family until the grapes grow dust on their
purple faces.
I'll take you to him.

EURYDICE

Now?

FATHER

It's for the best.

> *He takes her arm.*
> *They process, arm in arm, as at a wedding.*
> *Wedding music.*

They are solemn and glad.
They walk.
They see Orpheus up ahead.

Is that him?

EURYDICE

Yes—I think so—

FATHER

His shoulders aren't very broad. Can he take care of you?

Eurydice nods.

Are you sure?

EURYDICE

Yes.

FATHER

There's one thing you need to know. If he turns around and sees you, you'll die a second death. Those are the rules. So step quietly. And don't cry out.

EURYDICE

I won't.

FATHER

Good-bye.

They embrace.

EURYDICE

I'll come back to you. I seem to keep dying.

FATHER

Don't let them dip you in the River too long, the second time. Hold your breath.

EURYDICE

I'll look for a tree.

FATHER

I'll write you letters.

EURYDICE

Where will I find them?

FATHER

I don't know yet. I'll think of something. Good-bye, Eurydice.

EURYDICE

Good-bye.

> *They move away.*
> *The Father waves.*
> *She waves back,*
> *as though on an old steamer ship.*
> *The Father exits.*
> *Eurydice takes a deep breath.*
> *She takes a big step forward toward the audience,*
> *on an unseen gangplank.*
> *She is brave.*
> *She takes another step forward.*
> *She hesitates.*
> *She is all of a sudden not so brave.*
> *She is afraid.*
> *She looks back.*
> *She turns in the direction of her father,*
> *her back to the audience.*
> *He's out of sight.*

Wait, come back!

LITTLE STONE

You can't go back now, Eurydice.

EURYDICE

LOUD STONE

Face forward!

BIG STONE

Keep walking.

EURYDICE

I'm afraid!

LOUD STONE

Your husband is waiting for you, Eurydice.

EURYDICE

I don't recognize him! That's a stranger!

LITTLE STONE

Go on. It's him.

EURYDICE

I want to go home! I want my father!

LOUD STONE

You're all grown-up now. You have a husband.

THE STONES

TURN AROUND!

EURYDICE

Why?

THE STONES

BECAUSE!

EURYDICE

That's a stupid reason.

LITTLE STONE

Orpheus braved the gates of hell to find you.

LOUD STONE

He played the saddest music.

BIG STONE

Even we—

THE STONES

The stones—

LITTLE STONE

cried when we heard it.

Eurydice turns slowly, facing front.

EURYDICE

That's Orpheus?

THE STONES

Yes, that's him!

EURYDICE

Where's his music?

THE STONES

It's in your head.

*Orpheus walks slowly, in a straight line, with the
focus of a tightrope walker.
Eurydice moves to follow him. She follows him, several steps behind.
THEY WALK.
Eurydice follows him with precision, one step for every step he takes.
She makes a decision. She increases her pace.
She takes two steps for every step that Orpheus takes.
She catches up to him.*

EURYDICE

Orpheus?

He turns toward her, startled.
Orpheus looks at Eurydice.
Eurydice looks at Orpheus.
The world falls away.

ORPHEUS

You startled me.

A small sound—ping.
They turn their faces away from each other, matter-of-fact, compelled.
The lights turn blue.

EURYDICE

I'm sorry.

ORPHEUS

Why?

EURYDICE

I don't know.

Syncopated:

ORPHEUS

You always clapped your hands
on the third beat
you couldn't wait for the fourth.
Remember—
I tried to teach you—

you were always one step ahead
of the music
your sense of rhythm—
it was—off—

EURYDICE

I could never spell the word
rhythm—
it is such a difficult
word to spell—
r—y—no—there's an H in
it—
somewhere—a breath—
rhy—rhy—
rhy—

ORPHEUS

I would say clap on the downbeat—
no, the downbeat—

It's dangerous not
to have a sense of rhythm.
You *lose* things when you can't
keep a simple beat—
why'd you have to say my name—
Eurydice—

EURYDICE

I'm sorry.

ORPHEUS

I know we used to fight—
it seems so silly now—if—

EURYDICE

If ifs and ands were pots and pans
there'd be no need for tinkers—

ORPHEUS

Why?

*They begin walking away from each other
on extensive unseen boardwalks,
their figures long shadows,
looking straight ahead.*

EURYDICE

If ifs and ands were pots and pans
there'd be no need for tinkers—

ORPHEUS

Eurydice—

EURYDICE

I think I see the gates.
The stones—the boat—
it looks familiar—
the stones look happy to see me—

EURYDICE

ORPHEUS

Don't look—

EURYDICE

Wow! That's the happiest I've ever seen them!

Syncopated:

ORPHEUS	EURYDICE
Think of things we did	Everything is so gray—
	it looks familiar—
we went ice-skating—	like home—
	our house was—
I wore a red sweater—	gray—with a red door—
	we had two cats
	and two dogs
	and two fish
	that died—

ORPHEUS

Will you talk to me!

EURYDICE

The train looks like
the opposite of a train—

ORPHEUS

Eurydice!
WE'VE KNOWN EACH OTHER FOR CENTURIES!
I want to reminisce!
Remember when you wanted your name in a song
so I put your name in a song—
When I played my music
at the gates of hell
I was singing your name
over and over and over again.
Eurydice.

He grows quiet.
They walk away from each other on extended lines
until they are out of sight.

Scene 3

THE STONES

Finally.
Some peace.

LOUD STONE

And quiet.

THE STONES

Like the old days.
No music.
No conversation.
How about that.

A pause.

FATHER

With Eurydice gone it will be a second death for me.

LITTLE STONE

Oh, please, sir—

BIG STONE

We're tired.

FATHER

Do you understand the love a father has for his daughter?

LITTLE STONE

Love is a big, funny word.

BIG STONE

Dead people should be seen and not heard.

The Father looks at the Stones.
He looks at the string room.
He dismantles the string room,
matter-of-fact.
There's nothing else to do.
This can take time.
It takes time to dismantle a room made of string.
Music.
He sits down in what used to be the string room.

FATHER

How does a person remember to forget.
It's difficult.

LOUD STONE

It's not difficult.

LITTLE STONE

We told you how it works.

LOUD STONE

Dip yourself in the river.

BIG STONE

Dip yourself in the river.

LITTLE STONE

Dip yourself in the river.

FATHER

I need directions.

LOUD STONE

That's ridiculous.

BIG STONE

There are no directions.

A pause.
The Father thinks.

FATHER

I remember.
Take Tri-State South 294—
to Route 88 West.
Take Route 88 West to Route 80.
You'll go over a bridge.
Go three miles and you'll come
to the exit for Middle Road.
Proceed three to four miles.
Duck Creek Park will be on the right.
Take a left on Fernwood Avenue.
Continue straight on Fernwood past

two intersections.
Go straight.
Fernwood will curve to the right leading
you to Forest Road.
Take a left on Forest Road.
Go two blocks.
Pass the first entrance to the alley on the right.
Take the second entrance.
You'll go about a hundred yards.
A red brick house will
be on the right.
Look for Illinois license plates.

Go inside the house.
In the living room,
look out the window.
You'll see the lights on the Mississippi River.
Take off your shoes.
Walk down the hill.

You'll pass a tree good for climbing on the right.
Cross the road.
Watch for traffic.
Cross the train tracks.
Catfish are sleeping in the mud, on your left.
Roll up your jeans.
Count to ten.
Put your feet in the river
and swim.

> *He dips himself in the river.*
> *A small metallic sound of forgetfulness—ping.*
> *The sound of water.*
> *He lies down on the ground,*
> *curled up, asleep.*

> *Eurydice returns and sees that her string room is gone.*

EURYDICE

Where's my room?

> *The Stones are silent.*

(*To the Stones*) WHERE IS MY ROOM?
Answer me!

LITTLE STONE

It's none of our business.

LOUD STONE

What are you doing here?

BIG STONE

You should be with your husband.

LOUD STONE

Up there.

EURYDICE

Where's my father?

The Stones point to the Father.

(To the Stones) Why is he sleeping?

The Stones shrug their shoulders.

(To her father) I've come back!

LOUD STONE

He can't hear you.

LITTLE STONE

It's too late.

EURYDICE

What are you talking about?

BIG STONE

He dipped himself in the River.

EURYDICE

My father did not dip himself in the River.

THE STONES

He did!
We saw him!

LOUD STONE

He wanted some peace and quiet.

EURYDICE

(To the Stones) HE DID NOT!
(To her father) Listen. I'll teach you the words. Then we'll know each other again. Ready? We'll start with my name. Eurydice. E, U, R, Y . . .

BIG STONE

He can't hear you.

LOUD STONE

He can't see you.

LITTLE STONE

He can't remember you.

EURYDICE

(To the Stones) I hate you! I've always hated you!
Shut up! Shut up! Shut up!
(To her father) Listen. I'll tell you a story.

LITTLE STONE

He can't hear you.

BIG STONE

He can't see you.

LOUD STONE

He can't remember you.

LITTLE STONE

Try speaking in the language of stones.

LOUD STONE

It's a very quiet language.
Like if the pores in your
face opened up and wanted to talk.

EURYDICE

Stone.
Rock.
Tree. Rock. Stone.

> *It doesn't work.*
> *She holds her father.*

LOUD STONE

Didn't you already mourn for your father, young lady?

LITTLE STONE

Some things should be left well enough alone.

BIG STONE

To mourn twice is excessive.

LITTLE STONE

To mourn three times a sin.

LOUD STONE

Life is like a good meal.

BIG STONE

Only gluttons want more food when they finish their helping.

LITTLE STONE

Learn to be more moderate.

BIG STONE

It's weird for a dead person to be morbid.

LITTLE STONE

We don't like to watch it!

LOUD STONE

We don't like to see it!

BIG STONE

It makes me uncomfortable.

Eurydice cries.

THE STONES

Don't cry!
Don't cry!

BIG STONE

Learn the art of keeping busy!

EURYDICE

IT'S HARD TO KEEP BUSY WHEN YOU'RE DEAD!

THE STONES

It is not hard!
We keep busy
And we like it
We're busy busy busy stones
Watch us work
Keeping still
Keeping quiet
It's hard work
To be a stone
No time for crying.
No no no!

EURYDICE

I HATE YOU! I'VE ALWAYS HATED YOU!

She runs toward the Stones and tries to hit them.

THE STONES

Go ahead.
Try to hit us.

LITTLE STONE

You'll hurt your fist.

BIG STONE

You'll break your hand.

THE STONES

Ha ha ha!

Enter the child.
He has grown.
He is now at least ten feet tall.
His voice sounds suspiciously
like the Nasty Interesting Man's.

CHILD

Is there a problem here?

THE STONES

No, sir.

CHILD

(To Eurydice) You chose to stay with us, huh? Good.

He looks her over.

Perhaps to be my bride?

EURYDICE

I told you. You're too young.

CHILD

I'll be the judge of that.
I've grown.

EURYDICE

Yes—I see that.

CHILD

I'm ready to be a man now. I'm ready—to be—a man.

EURYDICE

Please. Leave me alone.

CHILD

I'll have them start preparing the satins and silks. You can't refuse
me. I've made my choice. I'm ready to be a man now.

EURYDICE

Can I have a moment to prepare myself?

CHILD

Don't be long. The wedding songs are already being written. They're very quiet. Inaudible, you might say. A dirt-filled orchestra for my bride. Don't trouble the songs with your music, I say. A song is two dead bodies rubbing under the covers to keep warm.

He exits.

THE STONES

Well, well, well!

LITTLE STONE

You had better prepare yourself.

EURYDICE

There is nothing to prepare.

BIG STONE

You had better comb your hair.

LOUD STONE

You had better find a veil.

EURYDICE

I don't need a veil. I need a pen!

LITTLE STONE

Pens are forbidden here.

EURYDICE

I need a pencil then.

LOUD STONE

Pencils, too.

EURYDICE

Damn you! I'll dip you in the River!

BIG STONE

Too late, too late!

EURYDICE

There must be a pen. There are. There must be.

She remembers the pen and paper in the breast pocket of her father's coat.
She takes them out.
She holds the pen up to show the Stones.
She gloats.

A pen.

She writes a letter:

Dear Orpheus,

I'm sorry. I don't know what came over me. I was afraid.
I'm not worthy of you. But I still love you, I think. Don't try
to find me again. You would be lonely for music. I want you
to be happy. I want you to marry again. I am going to write
out instructions for your next wife.

To My Husband's Next Wife:
Be gentle.
Be sure to comb his hair when it's wet.
Do not fail to notice
that his face flushes pink
like a bride's
when you kiss him.
Give him lots to eat.
He forgets to eat and he gets cranky.

When he's sad,
kiss his forehead and I will thank you.

Because he is a young prince
and his robes are too heavy on him.
His crown falls down
around his ears.
I'll give this letter to a worm. I hope he finds you.

Love,
Eurydice

She puts the letter on the ground.
She dips herself in the River.
A small metallic sound of forgetfulness—ping.
The sound of water.
She lies down next to her father, as though asleep.

The sound of an elevator—ding.
Orpheus appears in the elevator.
He sees Eurydice.
He is happy.
The elevator starts raining on Orpheus.
He forgets.
He steps out of the elevator.
He sees the letter on the ground.
He picks it up.
He scrutinizes it.
He can't read it.
He stands on it.
He closes his eyes.
The sound of water.
Then silence.

THE END

SARAH RUHL's plays include *The Clean House* (Pulitzer Prize Finalist, 2005; The Susan Smith Blackburn Prize, 2004); *Passion Play, a cycle* (The Fourth Freedom Forum Playwriting Award from The Kennedy Center, a Helen Hayes Awards nomination for best new play); *Melancholy Play*; *Eurydice*; *Orlando* and *Late: a cowboy song.* Upcoming productions include *The Clean House* at Lincoln Center Theater in New York City and *Demeter in the City* at Redcat in Los Angeles. Her plays have been produced at the Goodman Theatre, Arena Stage, the Woolly Mammoth Theatre Company, South Coast Repertory, Yale Repertory Theatre, Berkeley Repertory Theatre, The Wilma Theater, Actors Theatre of Louisville, Madison Repertory Theatre and the Piven Theatre, among others. Her plays have also been produced in London, Germany, Australia, Canada and Israel, and have been translated into Polish, Russian, Spanish, Norwegian, Korean and German. Originally from Chicago, Ms. Ruhl received her M.F.A. from Brown University where she studied with Paula Vogel. In 2003, she was the recipient of a Helen Merrill Emerging Playwrights Award and a Whiting Writers' Award. She is a member of 13P and New Dramatists.